A Glance at America

ちょっと見のアメリカ

Jack Brajcich

Toshihiro Tanioka

EIHŌSHA

は　じ　め　に

　本書は、平易な英語を通してアメリカ理解を深めると共に、英語の4技能（reading, listening, writing, speaking）の基礎力アップを目指す教材です。

　本書の主な特徴は以下のとおりです。

◆バランスの良い構成
・1ユニットは1演習（90分）で完結。時間配分はReading（passage）40分、Listening 15分、Writing 20分、Speaking（Dialog）10分が目安です。尚、プラスαとしてTOEIC®試験の問題形式の一つIncomplete Sentenceの練習問題も加えました。時間の余裕があれば挑戦してみてください。
　一応、毎時間、1ユニット完結を想定していますが、クラスの特徴により展開に工夫があってもよいと思います。例えば、1ユニットを2回／時間に分ける、Reading & Writingのクラスなら PassageとWritingのみを扱うのも一つの方法です。

◆Reading → 本文passageに関する紹介文と豊富な語（句）のヒント
・各ユニットは毎回、扱うトピックは独立しており、毎回の授業に新鮮な気持ちで取り組めます。そして、導入としてトピックに関する紹介文などを記載しています。また、語句のヒントも豊富にして辞書で単語を引く手間が省け、本文の内容把握により傾注できる読解重視の構成にしています。予習も効率よくできます。

◆Listening → TOEICと実用英語技能検定（英検）の設問形式
・英語の検定試験の代表的試験であるTOEICと英検（2級、準2級）の設問形式を模した設問。質問は文字にはせずに音声のみとし（英検形式）、文字のヒントが無いより聴解力を試す、伸ばす形式にしています。

◆Writing → 英語の基本文法に沿った表現力・英作力の養成（2部構成）
・英作問題は英文法の項目毎に2レベルの問題を配しました。語順を問う基礎問題と難度を上げて語彙、文法力、表現力を問う問題の2部構成にして、英作の苦手な者と基礎問題では物足りない者の両方に対応しています。

◆Speaking → Dialog（短い会話）の一部を書き取る形式
・使用頻度の高い役立つ英文ですので音声をお手本に暗記し使ってみましょう。書き取り対象の文章以外にも多くの活用度の高い表現を含みますので、CD音声を真似てDialog全てを丸暗記するのがベストです。

◆各ユニットのPromenade
・ユニット毎にPromenadeを配し、各Passageのタイトルや内容に関連するエピソード等を加えました。アメリカへの関心の伸長と共に、相乗効果的に更なる英語学習への動機づけになることも期待できます。

◆豊富な写真、イラスト、表など
・視覚面からも理解、関心、好奇心のアップが期待されます。なお、付録として巻

末に日米の概史、アメリカの歴代大統領名を付記しました。本文理解の一助になれば幸いです。

　外国語の学習は、その言語が母語である国々の文化についても一緒に学習することが肝要です。本書は、こうした視点からも編集し著わしました。アメリカが日本にとって、好むと好まざるとに無関係に最も関係の深い国の一つであることは事実です。そんなアメリカで 2021 年 1 月 6 日、連邦議会議事堂の襲撃事件が起こりました。民主主義への挑戦でした。民主主義国家の role model であるアメリカの一挙手一投足は、世界の耳目を集めます。

　本書が学生皆さんの英語力向上だけでなく、こうしたアメリカ理解の一助になることを願ってやみません。

　最後に、本書の出版にあたり、英宝社社長の佐々木元氏と、編集と校正段階などで大変お世話になった同社編集部の下村幸一氏に心から謝意を表します。コロナ禍でしたが予定通りに本書を上梓できて安堵しています。

2022 年（令和 4 年）晩秋　　著　者

A Glance at America
ちょっと見のアメリカ

CONTENTS（目　次）

Appendix

Unit 1 — The Star-Spangled Banner

アメリカ国旗
星条旗とも言われるアメリカ国旗は白、青、赤の３色。
白は純粋と潔白、赤は大胆さと勇気、青は忍耐と正義を意味する
と言われる。
※カラーの国旗は裏表紙を参照。

I Passage ♪2

◆ Words & Phrases

Take a close look at the American national flag above, the Star-Spangled **Banner**. It is sometimes called the *Stars and Stripes*, too. The number of **stripes**, thirteen, shows the initial number of **states** of the United States of America. Thirteen
5 British **colonies** on the present American east coast **declared independence** from Great Britain in 1776 and officially became independent in 1783. The number of stars, fifty, shows the current number of states. In the 19th century, twenty-nine **territories** became official states with expansion of the U.S.
10 **land mass** and sharp population **increase**. As the number of new states **increased**, so did the number of stars on the national flag.

In July 1960, the current banner was updated as it is now when Hawaii joined the United States of America as an official
15 state in August 1959. Although America acquired the Hawaiian Islands back in 1898, the Islands remained a territory for more than half a century. While the number of 13 stripes in the flag remains the same, the number of stars could be subject to change depending on the future **statehood** of the other U.S.
20 territories, such as Guam and Puerto Rico.

The Star-Spangled Banner is also the title of the U.S. **national anthem**. In the early 1810s, America fought the War of 1812 against Great Britain. Francis Scott Key, a Washington lawyer, was on a vessel near U.S. **Fort** McHenry near
25 Washington D.C. amid the war in 1814. The British soldiers **bombarded** the fort throughout the night **to no avail**. Seeing the American national flag still in place at dawn flying over the fort, Mr. Key was inspired to write a poem on the back of an envelope, which would later become the national anthem.
30 Winning the war, America made its independence much more **solid**.

The anthem is played or sung at various occasions, such as presidential **inaugurations** and major sporting events like the Super Bowl and the World Series, to name a few. It is a moment
35 of displaying faith and **patriotism** to the nation.

banner 旗
stripes しま、筋
states 州
colonies 植民地
declare 宣言する
independence 独立

territories 準州、領地
land mass 領土
increase 増加（する）

statehood 州

national anthem 国歌

fort 要塞

bombard 砲撃する
to no avail 失敗する

solid 堅固な

inauguration 就任式

patriotism 愛国心

Choose the correct answer about the passage.

  1 A   America officially became independent.

     B   America declared independence.

     C   No, it was in 1776.

     D   Twenty-nine territories became official states.

  2 A   a captain of a boat

     B   a lawyer

     C   a soldier

     D   on the back of an envelope

  3 A   Twenty-nine stars were newly added.

     B   simply because of a population increase in America

     C   Because American land was expanded and its population increased.

     D   in the early 1810s

  4 A   Hawaii is not a U.S. territory, but a state.

     B   Great Britain won the 1812 war.

     C   Mr. Key was glad to see the flag still flying over the fort.

     D   Guam is not a U.S. state.

Additional Listening Practice   ①

Choose the best response to the question or statement.

  1 A   B   C

  2 A   B   C

Exercise 1　［　　］内の語（句）を並べ替え日本文にあう英文を書きなさい。
（注：句読点等は要適宜対応）

1　この前の日曜日、君は家にいましたか。　［at, last, were, Sunday, you, home］

_____

2　リビングのテーブルの下に2匹の猫がいます。

　　　　　　［two, room, under, in, are, the living, cats, there, table, the］

_____

3　僕らはお腹が空いているけど夕食の準備はまだできていない。

　　　　　　［is, hungry, not, we, but, ready, dinner, yet, are］

_____

Exercise 2　次の各日本文にあう英文を **be 動詞**に注意して書いてみましょう。

1　スミス氏はボストン出身で、彼はとても有名なピアニストです。

　→ _____

2　彼の両親は大学教授です。父親はアメリカ人でハワイ生まれです。

　→ _____

3　10年前、この市にはホテルは2つしかなかった。

　→ _____

Incomplete Sentence → Reading Section の文中下線に入る適語（句）を選ぶ問題に挑戦しよう！

A word or phrase is missing in each of the sentences below. Select the best answer to complete the sentence.

1　The big box was ＿＿＿ for me to move and I needed someone to help me move it.

　　A　too heavy　　B　too heavily　　C　so heavy　　D　such heavy

2　When I entered my daughter's room, she was ＿＿＿ to the radio in her bed.

　　A　to listen　　B　being listened　　C　to be listening　　D　listening

3　My father often ＿＿＿ me with my English homework when I was a freshman in high school.

　　A　helps　　B　has assisted　　C　helped　　D　had assisted

4　Two of us have known ＿＿＿ over twenty years. We were roommates in the college dorm.

　　A　with each other　　B　each other　　C　to each other　　D　by each other

5　It will take some time to cause damage for sanctions ＿＿＿ on Russian by America and its allies.

　　A　imposed　　B　has imposed　　C　were imposed　　D　imposing

［A：customs inspector　B：traveler］

A：May I see your passport?

B：＿＿＿＿＿　＿＿＿＿＿　＿＿＿＿＿.

A：What's the purpose of your visit?

B：Sightseeing.　＿＿＿＿＿　＿＿＿＿＿　＿＿＿＿＿　＿＿＿＿＿.

A：How long are you going to stay?

B：＿＿＿＿＿　＿＿＿＿＿　＿＿＿＿＿.

A：Fine.　＿＿＿＿＿　＿＿＿＿＿　＿＿＿＿＿.

Promenade 1

アメリカ南部連合国家の国旗

アメリカは 1861 年から 1865 年まで国を北部と南部に 2 分する南北戦争（the Civil War）を戦った。開戦後、南部諸州のアメリカ連合国は左のような独自の国旗を作った。合衆国を脱退した南部の州の数は 13 州でアメリカ建国時の州の数と同じだった。今日でも南部の一部には同旗を色々な機会に掲げる地区や個人もいる。

なお同戦争は北部が勝利し争点だった奴隷制度は廃止された。

U.S. Time Zones

国内時差

日本の面積の25倍の広さのアメリカ。

全国一律、同時間とはいかないようです。

アメリカは日本で言うサマータイムも導入しているのでこちらも要注意です。

因みにサマータイムにあたる英語は、daylight saving time

I Passage 〔5〕

◆ Words & Phrases

America has fifty states and it is about twenty-five times larger than Japan in size. Alaska is the largest state, Texas the second and California the third. The size of California is a little larger than that of Japan. Its **mainland** spreads from the

5　Atlantic Ocean to the Pacific Ocean. Located close to **the Arctic** and purchased from Russia in 1867, Alaska is northwest from the mainland America. The state of Hawaii, **consisting of** the Hawaiian Islands, is about three thousand miles apart from Los Angeles on the west coast. This large size of American **land**

10　**mass** makes it **inevitable** to set separate time zones.

America has basically six time zones. They are the Eastern Standard, the Central Standard, the Mountain Standard, the Pacific Standard, the Alaska Standard, and the Hawaii Standard. The nation's capital Washington D.C., New York and Atlanta

15　are in the Eastern time zone. Chicago, New Orleans, and Houston are in the Central, Denver and Salt Lake City are in the Mountain. San Francisco, Las Vegas and Los Angeles are in the Pacific. Los Angeles is three hours behind New York. Anchorage, Alaska is one hour and Honolulu in Hawaii are two

20　hours behind Los Angeles respectively. No major TV company starts **broadcasting** their evening news **mentioning** exactly what time it is because the time varies from area to area. CBS, one of the major U.S.TV corporations, starts its evening news program saying *CBS Evening News*. So does another major TV

25　corporation, ABC does by saying *World News Tonight*.

When you travel or plan touring in America, check the time difference. When you fly from Washington D.C. to San Francisco, you will reach San Francisco three hours later even though you spend about six hours on board. You will arrive in

30　D.C. nine hours later if travelling the other way around! Also, see to it what time it is in the American city when you make an **overseas** call from Japan to your friends, family members, and business customers there.

mainland 本土

the Arctic 北極

consisting of ～から成る

land mass 面積、領土
inevitable 必然

broadcasting 放送する
mention 述べる

overseas 海外への

8

Choose the correct answer about the passage.

1 A   It is in the Pacific time zone.

   B   the west coast

   C   No, both Alaska and Texas are larger than Japan.

   D   California

2 A   two hours

   B   Yes, both are one hour behind Alaska.

   C   It is not clear from the passage.

   D   three hours

3 A   It is a TV company in Washington D.C.

   B   No, it is CBS.

   C   Its evening news is *World News Tonight*.

   D   Yes, it is sometimes light even in the evening.

4 A   Hawaiians may be having breakfast when New Yorkers are having lunch.

   B   Russia sold the Hawaiian Islands to America.

   C   You spend nine hours on board if you fly from San Francisco to the U.S. capital.

   D   Alaska is on the west coast.

Additional Listening Practice   ②

Listen to two short conversations and choose the best answers for the questions.

1 A   He got well.

   B   He will major in medicine in college.

   C   He will buy some new headsets.

   D   He will go to see a doctor.

2 A   on the street

   B   on the phone

   C   in Bob's car

   D   at the post office

Ⅲ　Writing　②　時制 1　現在形

Exercise 1 ［　　］内の語（句）を並べ替え日本文にあう英文を書きなさい。
（注：句読点等は要適宜対応）

1　私の祖父は毎朝、その公園を散歩します。

［takes, the park, my, a walk, in, morning, grandpa, every］

_____

2　私の兄が帰宅するまで私とここにいなさい。

［my brother, home, with, until, here, me, comes, stay］

_____

3　父はタバコは吸いませんが、たまにビールは飲みます。

［drinks, he, once, a, smoke, doesn't, my father, while, but, beer, in］

_____

Exercise 2　次の各日本文にあう英文を**動詞の時制（現在形）**に注意して書いてみましょう。

1　母は花が大好きで、庭で沢山のバラやチューリップを育てています。

→ _____

2　スミス先生はカナダ出身で、その語学学校で英語とフランス語を教えています。

→ _____

3　この地は、冬は毎年雪が降りますが、夏はあまり暑くなりません。

→ _____

Ⅳ　TOEIC® ②
Incomplete Sentence → Reading Section の文中下線に入る適語（句）を選ぶ問題に挑戦しよう！

A word or phrase is missing in each of the sentences below. Select the best answer to complete the sentence.

1　This morning I got up thirty minutes ＿＿＿ than usual to make breakfast for my mother.

A　earlier　　B　early　　C　be earlier　　D　much early

2　"I can drive you ＿＿＿ to the station." "That'll be a big help."

A　distant　　B　as far as　　C　as long as　　D　until

3　"May I ask a favor ＿＿＿ you?" "I'll be glad to do it if I can. What is it?"

A　to　　B　of　　C　for　　D　by

4　The interviewer ＿＿＿ me whether I had been abroad in my college days.

A　told　　B　asked　　C　said to　　D　spoke

5　It is eleven thirty now. It is high time you ＿＿＿ in bed.

A　be　　B　are　　C　went　　D　were

Fill in the blanks.
（CD を聴き空白部分を書き取り暗記しましょう。）

［A：hotel clerk　B：Japanese traveler〕

A：Good evening, sir. ＿＿＿＿＿ ＿＿＿＿＿ ＿＿＿＿＿ ＿＿＿＿＿?

B：Yes, I have a reservation. My name is Kenji Sato.

A：＿＿＿＿＿ ＿＿＿＿＿ ＿＿＿＿＿ ＿＿＿＿＿ ＿＿＿＿＿ again, please?

B：Sato, it's S-A-T-O.

A：Thank you very much. Yes, Mr. Sato. We have your reservation.

Will you fill out this form, please?

B：Sure. （*A few minutes later*） ＿＿＿＿＿ ＿＿＿＿＿ ＿＿＿＿＿.

A：Thank you, sir. ＿＿＿＿＿ ＿＿＿＿＿ ＿＿＿＿＿ ＿＿＿＿＿?

B：With my card.

Promenade 2

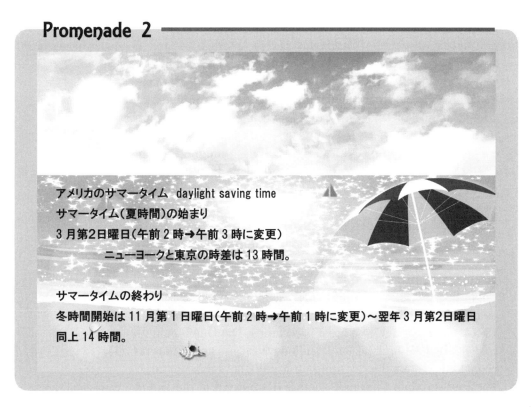

アメリカのサマータイム　daylight saving time

サマータイム（夏時間）の始まり

3 月第2日曜日（午前 2 時➡午前 3 時に変更）

　　　ニューヨークと東京の時差は 13 時間。

サマータイムの終わり

冬時間開始は 11 月第 1 日曜日（午前 2 時➡午前 1 時に変更）〜翌年 3 月第2日曜日

同上 14 時間。

Unit 3 — Welcome to New York

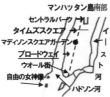

Winter Garden Theatre

ブロードウェイ（右地図南北点線）

ニューヨーク市の中心マンハッタン島を南北約54km を縦断する通り。ただ一般には Times Square を含む一画を構成する劇場街、ミュージカルの代名詞。

周辺には Carnegie Hall, Tiffany など。

I　Passage　🎧 8　　　　　　　　　◆ Words & Phrases

　　　Welcome to New York, America's largest city. Learn more about this city by touring along Broadway. Broadway is the center of **finance**, business, sightseeing and the **theatrical district** of New York. It starts at the southern edge of
5　Manhattan Island. Nearby are Ground Zero, City Hall, St. Paul's Chapel, Chinatown, **New York Stock Exchange**, and Wall Street, the original wall provided to protect against then called "Indians". Also nearby is Battery Park where the ferry to the Statue of Liberty and Ellis Island is **available**. Broadway
10　extends north up along famous **venues** and sites, such as Central Park at 59th Street and at 116th Street is Columbia University, an Ivy League school.

　　　The exciting spot above all is Times Square and its **vicinity**. The name 'Times' comes from the *New York Times* whose
15　**headquarters** used to be there. The paper enjoys fame as a **quality paper** with the *Washington Post* in America. Located at the intersection of Seventh Avenue, Broadway, and 42nd Street, Times Square attracts tens of millions of visitors yearly from home and abroad. In its vicinity are Carnegie Hall, St. Patrick's
20　Cathedral, Rockefeller Center, and Madison Square Garden, an indoor arena for various events such as NBA games and concerts. At 33rd Street is the Empire State Building. Built in 1931, the 102-story **skyscraper** was the tallest building in the world for about four decades, a symbol of the growing city of
25　New York. At 50th Street is the Winter Garden Theatre where the musical *Cats* debuted in 1982. Times Square draws global attention at the time of the ball drop to celebrate the New Year.

　　　Naming of New York also started on Broadway. After the discovery of the new continent of America by Christopher
30　Columbus in 1492, several European nations started building **colonies** on the continent. Great Britain, starting in 1607, built 13 colonies along the east coast of America. The Dutch built its colony, New Netherland later building New Amsterdam as its capital village, for the fur trade on Manhattan Island in 1612.
35　The English king, Charles II, feeling **distasteful** of the Dutch

finance 金融
theatrical district 劇場街
New York Stock Exchange ニューヨーク証券取引所
available （船が）出ている
venues 開催場所

vicinity 近郊

headquarters 本社
quality paper 有力紙

skyscraper 高層ビル

colonies 植民地

distasteful 嫌った

colony located alongside British colonies, took it in the mid 17th
century. The king **granted** the new colony to his brother, the   **granted** 与えた
Duke of York, who renamed it New York.

| **II** | **Listening Comprehension** 🎧 9 🎧 |

Choose the correct answer about the passage.

1 A at the southern edge of Manhattan Island
   B They celebrate the New Year there.
   C at the intersection of Broadway and 7th Avenue
   D The *New York Times* headquarters was.

2 A No, it is at 59th Street.
   B The musical *Cats* debuted at the Winter Garden Theatre.
   C The Empire State Building was built.
   D Carnegie Hall was built near Times Square.

3 A to the area near Wall Street
   B as a high quality newspaper
   C Because the area gets noisy at the time of New Year.
   D It is not clear from the passage.

4 A Columbia University is along Broadway but is not close to Times Square.
   B The ferry to the Statue of Liberty leaves from Central Park.
   C The Dutch built its colony in 1607.
   D Madison Square Garden is very close to Wall Street.

Additional Listening Practice   ③
Choose the best response to the question or statement.

1 A   B   C
2 A   B   C

Ⅲ Writing ③ 時制2 過去形＆未来形

Exercise 1 ［　　］内の語（句）を並べ替え日本文にあう英文を書きなさい。
（注：句読点等は要適宜対応）

1 トムは今日の午後、友人達とゴルフをするつもりです。

[this, with, Tom, play golf, afternoon, his, will, friends]

_____

2 我々はドアの前で奇妙な音を聞きました。

[a, heard, in, door, we, sound, the, front, strange, of]

_____

3 私は昨夜、寝る前に両親に手紙を書いた。

[before, a letter, to, I, bed, night, going, my parents, last, wrote, to]

_____

Exercise 2 次の各日本文にあう英文を**動詞の時制（過去形、未来形）**に注意して書いてみましょう。

1 僕はトムがこの週末、家にいるか知らない。　　　　　　　　［～か（どうか）☞ if］

　→ _____

2 私は海外旅行が好きです。去年は、ロンドンを訪問しました。今年は、ニューヨークに行く予定です。　　　　　　　　　［海外を旅行する ☞ travel abroad］

　→ _____

3 僕のホストファミリーは日没後、その公園にジョギングには行かないようにと助言してくれた。　　　　　　　　　　　　　　　［日没後 ☞ after dark］

　→ _____

Ⅳ TOEIC® ③
Incomplete Sentence → Reading Section の文中下線に入る適語（句）を選ぶ問題に挑戦しよう！

A word or phrase is missing in each of the sentences below. Select the best answer to complete the sentence.

1 Tom and Tomoko _____ each other since they met at college in 1985.

　　A have known　　B has known　　C have been known　　D knew

2 I saw two men come out of the house and they drove away in their _____ cars.

　　A respectable　　B respecting　　C respectful　　D respective

3 Whatever you say, it won't _____ any difference to me.

　　A make　　B do　　C have　D bring

4 The peace talks in the Middle East have been quite _____ this year.

　　A succeeded　　B successful　　C succeeding　　D successive

5 After a short break, the party _____ its journey.

　　A recovered　　B resumed　　C removed　　D recalled

V   Dialog ③ 🎧 10
Fill in the blanks.
（CD を聴き空白部分を書き取り暗記しましょう。）

[A：hotel staff　B：guest]

A：Front desk. ＿＿＿＿＿＿ ＿＿＿＿＿＿ ＿＿＿＿＿＿ ＿＿＿＿＿＿?

B：Yes, this is Sato in room 721. ＿＿＿＿＿ ＿＿＿＿＿ ＿＿＿＿＿ ＿＿＿＿.

A：Oh, what is it, sir?

B：I'm afraid ＿＿＿＿＿ ＿＿＿＿ ＿＿＿＿ ＿＿＿＿ ＿＿＿＿ ＿＿＿＿.

A：＿＿＿＿＿ ＿＿＿＿＿ ＿＿＿＿＿ right away. We're sorry for the inconvenience.

B：That's all right.

Promenade 3
アメリカの象徴　自由の女神像（世界遺産）

ニューヨークと言えば自由の女神像。像も台座も各々約50mの高さがあり全体で約100ｍの高さの像。左手には独立宣言書を持ち自由を勝ち得た証であり、独立を支援したフランスの独立革命（1789年）に影響を与えた。右手には松明を掲げてアメリカへの移住を希望してニューヨークに着いた移民を歓迎してきた。

移民審査所当時のエリス島

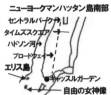

ニューヨークマンハッタン島南部
セントラルパーク
タイムズスクエア
ハドソン河
ブロードウェイ
エリス島
キャッスルガーデン
自由の女神像

移民の国の移民審査所

移民の国と言われるアメリカ。その審査所は、ニューヨークほかボストンやサンフランシスコにもあった。移民の入国ルートが海から空に変った20世紀半ば、各々その役割を終えた。

I   Passage 🎧 11   ◆ Words & Phrases

In the New York Harbor, there are two famous islands, Liberty Island and Ellis Island. On the former is **the Statue of Liberty**, well-known worldwide as a symbolic American monument. Located less than a mile away from Liberty Island is

5　Ellis Island, where there used to be the **immigrant** processing center. Before they started **inspecting** immigrants at Ellis Island, they inspected newcomers at Castle Garden at the southern edge of Manhattan in New York City. Toward the end of the 19th century, the number of immigrants coming to New

10　York became more than Castle Garden could **handle**. In January 1892, Ellis Island took over the role of inspecting the immigrants.

Ellis Island served as a **gateway** to America for the coming sixty-two years. Many immigrants from Europe in the late 19th

15　century and in the first half of the 20th century crossed the Atlantic and landed on Ellis Island. They looked at the Statue of Liberty from their vessels. For them, Ellis Island was a golden gate to the land of dreams, opportunity, hope, and freedom from **oppression** in their homelands.

20　Ellis Island was full of scenes and moments of joys, excitement, sadness and **despair** daily. Immigrants were subject to **medical checkups** as well as various questions such as their names, nationalities, destinations, and the amount of money they had. Due to the language barrier between the

25　**inspector** and some immigrants, the inspector sometimes recorded immigrants' home countries as their names. Although a few aliens were not **admitted**, most were accepted, among whom were two Nobel **laureates**, the physicist Albert Einstein and the writer Thomas Mann. While some stayed in New York,

30　many spread across the nation.

The center caught on fire in June 1897. All the records were burned to ashes but no one was hurt. Re-built in 1900, the center started inspections again. Ellis Island inspected nearly 12 million immigrants in total. After the center was closed in 1954,

35　the U.S. government tried to sell Ellis Island but no one was

the Statue of Liberty 自由の女神像

immigrant 移民
inspect 検査する

handle 処理する

gateway 玄関

oppression 抑圧

despair 絶望
medical checkups 健康診断

inspector 検査官

admit 受け入れる
laureates 受賞者

interested. It is now part of a national park and attracts many tourists. No one is turned away.

Ⅱ Listening Comprehension

Choose the correct answer about the passage.

1 A at the southern edge of Manhattan
   B in the Atlantic
   C in the New York Harbor
   D Many came there from Europe.

2 A The processing center was closed in 1954.
   B more than sixty years
   C Not all aliens were accepted.
   D as a gateway to the land of freedom

3 A part of the national park
   B Because it was near the Statue of Liberty.
   C The number of aliens coming to New York rose.
   D Nobody was interested in buying it.

4 A how much money they had
   B the name of the port in Europe they boarded the ship
   C name and birthplace
   D the name of the place they are headed for

Additional Listening Practice ④

Listen to two short conversations and choose the best answers for the questions.

1 A The show is about to start.   B about the boots in a case
   C at a shoe store   D The customer did not buy anything.

2 A He is Rose's husband.   B Mark will go to Tokyo next week.
   C Mark likes sweets.   D He has a nice rose garden.

Ⅲ　Writing　④　助動詞

Exercise 1　[　　] 内の語（句）を並べ替え日本文にあう英文を書きなさい。
（注：句読点等は要適宜対応）

1　今日の午後、君の自転車を貸してもらえないか？

[use, bicycle, this, your, I, may, afternoon]

_____

2　何時間も勉強して息子は疲れているに違いない。

[hours, tired, my son, for, after, be, must, studying]

_____

3　私は明日、3時に駅で彼女に会うつもりです。

[will, her, the, at three, tomorrow, at, I, station, meet]

_____

Exercise 2　次の各日本文にあう英文を**助動詞（can, may, must, will 等）**に注意して書いてみましょう。

1　風邪を引いたみたいです。帰宅してもいいですか。
　　→ _____

2　もう少し大きな声で話していただけませんか。（私は）君の言うこと / 君の声が
　　聞こえません。　　　　　　　　　　　　　　[大きい声で ☞ louder]
　　→ _____

3　明朝、始発のバスに乗るために、私は今夜は早く寝なければなりません。
　　→ _____

Ⅳ　TOEIC® ④
Incomplete Sentence → Reading Section の文中下線に入る適語（句）を選ぶ問題に挑戦しよう！

A word or phrase is missing in each of the sentences below. Select the best answer to complete the sentence.

1　The football game was a close one and we all ＿＿＿.

　　A　got exciting　　B　was excited　　C　got excited　　D　were exciting

2　Tom as well as his parents ＿＿＿ to the party scheduled for this weekend.

　　A　to be invited　　B　is invited　　C　are invited　　D　being invited

3　"What kind of necktie are you ＿＿＿ for, sir?"

　　A　be looking　　B　looked　　C　look　　D　looking

4　The candidate was busy preparing a speech for the press conference while ＿＿＿ the vote return.

　　A　waited　　B　waiting for　　C　waited for　　D　was waiting for

5　"Have you ever been abroad?" "No, ＿＿＿."

　　A　I have never　　B　have I never　　C　I never have　　D　have I not ever

V Dialog ④ 🎧13
Fill in the blanks.
（CD を聴き空白部分を書き取り暗記しましょう。）

［A：shop staff　B：customer］

A：Hi. ＿＿＿＿＿ ＿＿＿＿＿ ＿＿＿＿＿ ＿＿＿＿＿ ＿＿＿＿＿?

B：A Big Mac, large French fries, onion rings and a diet Coke.

A：＿＿＿＿＿ ＿＿＿＿＿ ＿＿＿＿＿ do you want?

B：Large, please.

A：Is that ＿＿＿＿＿ ＿＿＿＿＿ ＿＿＿＿＿ ＿＿＿＿＿ ＿＿＿＿＿?

B：For here.

A：That's $12.75.

B：＿＿＿＿＿ ＿＿＿＿＿ ＿＿＿＿＿

A：Out of fifteen. ＿＿＿＿＿ ＿＿＿＿＿ ＿＿＿＿＿. Have a nice day.

Promenade 4

エリス島
アメリカに入国が認められない者
アメリカ移民・帰化法の Section. 212 には入国が認められない者として下記のような者が列挙されている。

現在のエリス島

犯罪に関連のある者
・過去 1 年以内に入国を拒否された者（事前許可あれば可）
・過去においてアメリカ国内で逮捕され国外退去処分にあった者（同上）

思想面で問題視される者
・無政府主義者　　・一夫多妻制主義者
＊かつては共産主義者やその支持者、又は関係があると思われる者も認められなかった。その一人にイギリスの喜劇王チャーリー・チャップリンもいた。

その他
・感染性の保菌者　　・麻薬依存症の者
・アルコール依存症の者
・売春行為に関わったことのある者、またはそういう目的で入国しようとする者
・公的扶養の対象になる可能性が高いと認められる者

19

The Pulitzer Prize

ジャーナリズム界最高の賞ピューリッツァー賞
ベトナム戦争を扱った日本人ジャーナリストの写真家沢田教一。
34歳で夭折した沢田はベトナムの戦場を駆け巡り、真実を写真
で撮影しつづけた。ピューリッツァー賞をとった彼の戦場で撮っ
た左写真「安全への逃避」(1966年) は特に有名。

「安全への逃避」と沢田

I　Passage　14　◆ Words & Phrases

Columbia University in New York City announces the winners of the Pulitzer Prize in May every year. The prize is awarded to journalists including photographers, writers and artists for their excellent work. The name comes from Joseph
5　Pulitzer, a Jewish Hungarian, who came to Boston at the age of seventeen in 1864. Born in a wealthy family and well educated, Pulitzer left home touring around Europe to be a soldier. Pulitzer was unable to join any military mainly **due to** his weak eyesight and **delicate physique**. Fortunately, he was recruited
10　in Germany by an agent hiring soldiers to fight for **the North** in the **ongoing** American **Civil War**.

After leaving the military, Pulitzer moved to St. Louis in 1865. He **engaged** in various jobs such as a waiter, an **unloader** and an assistant for a lawyer, none of which lasted long. **Inspired**
15　by his last job, Pulitzer studied law and became a lawyer. He worked hard as a lawyer but his limited English **alienated** his clients. The turning point in his life came soon. A year after becoming a U.S. citizen, in 1868 at the age of 21, he got a job as a reporter for a local newspaper, his debut in the journalism
20　world. In 1878, he bought a local newspaper, the *St. Louis Dispatch*. However, Pulitzer moved to New York several years later.

In New York, Pulitzer raised his name as a **publisher**. In 1883, he bought the newspaper *World*. Rivalry with William
25　Hearst, the owner of the *New York Journal*, helped him grow and succeed as a publisher. They competed for more **circulation**, especially in reporting the Spanish-American War over Cuba.

Pulitzer is more remembered for promoting journalism. In
30　1903, he **endowed** $500,000 to Columbia University proposing to found the School of Journalism to educate professional journalists as well as to create the Pulitzer Prize. The school accepted 79 students in September 1912, one year after

due to ～が原因で
delicate physique
細身
the North 北部
ongoing 進行中の
Civil War
南北戦争 P.7 参照
engage 携わる
unloader（船荷）人夫
inspired 刺激を受け
て
alienate 遠ざける

publisher 新聞社主

circulation 販売部数

endow 寄付する

Pulitzer's death. In 1917, the first Pulitzer Prizes were awarded. Currently, the prize is **annually** awarded across over twenty categories. Pulitzer left a legacy for the nation which accepted him as an immigrant.

annually 每年

Ⅱ　Listening Comprehension

Choose the correct answer about the passage.

1 A Germany
  B Hungary
  C St. Louis
  D Boston

2 A in 1868
  B It was in 1867.
  C Yes, he was twenty-one years old.
  D when he was seventeen

3 A as a publisher
  B to be the owner of the paper *World*
  C to attend Columbia University
  D It is not clear from the passage.

4 A No, it was in 1917.
  B He taught 79 students at Columbia.
  C He gave lots of money to Columbia University.
  D the School of Journalism

Additional Listening Practice ⑤

Choose the best response to the question or statement.

1 A　　B　　C
2 A　　B　　C

Ⅲ Writing ⑤ 進行形

Exercise 1 ［　　］内の語（句）を並べ替え日本文にあう英文を書きなさい。
（注：句読点等は要適宜対応）

1　父は今、家の前で車を洗っています。

［in, is, the, of, washing, front, now, house, his car, my father］

_____

2　私が帰宅した時、母と姉は台所で料理をしていました。

When［cooking, my mother, sister, in, were, I, and, the kitchen, came home］

_____

3　兄は雨が激しく降っていたので、その時はゆっくり運転していた。

［was, because, hard, driving, was, it, my brother, then, slowly, raining］

_____

Exercise 2　次の各日本文にあう英文を**進行形（be 動詞＋動詞 ing 形）**に注意して書いてみましょう。

1　雨が激しく降り始めた時、我々はその公園で野球をしていました。

→ _____

2　「ここで何をしているの？」「財布を探しています。」　［～を探す ☞ look for ～］

→ _____

3　「明日の今頃は何をしているの？」「英語の試験を受けているよ。」

［明日の今頃 ☞ at this time tomorrow］

→ _____

Ⅳ TOEIC® ⑤
Incomplete Sentence → Reading Section の文中下線に入る適語（句）を選ぶ問題に挑戦しよう！

A word or phrase is missing in each of the sentences below. Select the best answer to complete the sentence.

1　We will have an entrance exam next month and our teacher always ＿＿＿ us to study hard.

A　tells　　B　speaks　　C　says　　D　talks

2　It seems that soccer has become as ＿＿＿ as baseball among young Japanese.

A　popularity　　B　popular　　C　more popular　　D　very popular

3　Mark ＿＿＿ but he kept on walking till he came to a small hotel.

A　was tired　　B　had been tiring　　C　was being tired　　D　would be tiring

4　These are ＿＿＿ my grandpa used to wear when he read papers.

A　a pair of glass　　B　the glasses　　C　the glass　　D　glasses

5　"Will you ＿＿＿ able to finish the work by tomorrow evening?" "I'll do my best."

A　be　　B　are　　C　been　　D　being

V Dialog ⑤ 🎧 16
Fill in the blanks.
（CD を聴き空白部分を書き取り暗記しましょう。）

[A：Japanese traveler　B：stranger]

A：Excuse me, but _____ _____ _____ _____?

B：Sure, if I can. _____ _____ _____?

A：_____ _____. How can I get to the Hilton Hotel?

B：It's just around that corner. It'll be on your left.

_____ _____ _____ _____.

A：Thank you so much.

B：Not at all.

Promenade 5

ピューリッツァー賞

ジャーナリズム界最高の賞ピューリッツァー賞の創設者のピューリッツァー（左写真の左中央）は、もう一つレガシーを残した。

19世紀後半、フランスから自由の女神像が米国に寄贈されることになった。しかし、その台座は米国自前で建設が必要となった。1885年、ピューリッツァーは自らが社主を務めるWorld紙で台座建設のための寄付を募った（左写真）。約12万人から10万ドルの寄付が寄せられ1886年、現在の場所に設置された女神像。自由と移民歓迎の象徴としてニューヨーク港に佇む。

ピューリッツァーを移民とし受け入れたアメリカへの恩返しだったのかもしれない。

Unit 6 Give Me Your Best and Brightest

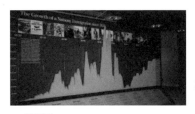

アメリカへの移民数は今世紀に入り毎年、70万人（2003年）から127万人（2006年）と平均で年100万人近い数となっている。アメリカは今も"黄金の地"の顔を持つ国なのです。

左写真：米国への移民数推移を示すパネル（エリス島博物館）
中央右の落ち込みは大恐慌と第二次世界大戦が主因。

I Passage 17

◆ Words & Phrases

America is a nation of **immigrants**. As of 2020, America accepted about eighty-seven million newcomers. America has preferably accepted two types of immigrants. One is that of a family reunion for **spouses**, children and **siblings** of U.S.
5 citizens and **green card holders**. The other is the employment-based **preference** to accept experts with the **advanced** degrees or exceptional abilities and skilled workers. Both **cherishing** family ties and accepting the best and brightest have been the **well established** U.S. policy for a century since
10 the 1920s.

"American and two Japanese Physicists shared Nobel for work on LED lights." So went an article in the New York Times in October 2014. Japan's media, on the other hand, reported that *three* Japanese won the Nobel Prize. '*American*' in the
15 Times referred to Shuji Nakamura at the University of California, Santa Barbara. Nakamura, a native Japanese, became a U.S. citizen in 2005. In 2021, the Nobel Prize was awarded to Dr. Shukuro Manabe of the U. S., a physicist and a native Japanese who became a U.S. citizen in 1975.

20 America has greatly benefited from **immigration**. Including the **eminent** physicist Albert Einstein, immigrants consist of 108 of the 310 U.S. Nobel Prize winners in chemistry, physics, and medicine in the period from 1901 to 2021. Limiting the period from 2001 to 2021, 33 of 94 U.S. **Nobel laureates** in
25 natural science including Nakamura and Manabe were foreign-born. In the same period, America accepted over 880,000 professional, highly educated, talented and skilled aliens. While the emigrant nations suffer from the "**brain drain**", America has benefited from the brain gain by proactively accepting the
30 talented immigrants.

Immigration has been an **asset** for America. Henry Kissinger from Germany and Madeleine Albright from Czechoslovakia, the first female **secretary of state**, served for their adopted nation as **prominent** diplomats. Among the foreign-born
35 celebrities are Michael J. Fox, Arnold Schwarzenegger, Billy

immigrant 移民

spouse 配偶者
siblings 兄弟姉妹
green card holders 永住権所有の外国人
preference 優先
advanced 高度な
cherish 大切にする
well established しっかり根付いた

immigration 移民
eminent 著名な

Nobel laureates ノーベル賞受賞者

brain drain 頭脳流出

asset 財産

secretary of state 国務長官
prominent 著名な

Idol, and Nadia Comăneci, to name a few. America has developed with the help of immigrants.

Ⅱ Listening Comprehension 🎧18

Choose the correct answer about the passage.

1 A in the early 20th century
   B in the period from 1901 to 2021
   C thirty-three in the 21st century
   D about 87 million

2 A a professor of physics at the University of California, Santa Barbara
   B He is an American citizen.
   C He won the Nobel Prize in the 20th century.
   D one of the three inventors of the LED lights

3 A one
   B none
   C two Japanese
   D three in October 2014

4 A The number of Nobel Prize winners in economics is not listed here.
   B Albert Einstein was a chemist.
   C Henry Kissinger was a foreign-born diplomat.
   D Family members of U.S. citizens are favorably accepted.

Additional Listening Practice ⑥

Listen to two short conversations and choose the best answers for the questions.

1 A by the computer in the man's house   B on the desk in the office
   C The man's computer is a desk top.   D He lost it at lunch time.

2 A They are going to buy some CDs and books.   B at a CD rental shop
   C in a music café   D It's not clear from their talk.

Ⅲ　Writing　⑥　受動態

Exercise 1 　[　　]内の語（句）を並べ替え日本文にあう英文を書きなさい。
（注：句読点等は要適宜対応）

1　アメリカは 1492 年にコロンブスによって発見された。

[was, America, in, discovered, 1492, Columbus, by]

_____

2　その光景には本当に驚きました。　　[at, the, I, really, was, scene, surprised]

_____

3　今朝、私が起きた時、庭は雪でおおわれていた。

[got, when, was, the garden, covered, this, with, I, up, morning, snow]

Exercise 2 　次の各日本文にあう英文を**受動態（be 動詞＋過去分詞＋by 等）**に注意して書いてみましょう。

1　僕は、その白い車にはねられた直後に、この病院に搬送された。

→ _____

2　私の両親は妹がサッカーに関心があると聞いて驚いています。

→ _____

3　私の息子は島のほとんどの人が知っているその新しい若い医者に治療を受けた。

→ _____

Ⅳ　TOEIC® ⑥

Incomplete Sentence → Reading Section の文中下線に入る適語（句）を選ぶ問題に挑戦しよう！

A word or phrase is missing in each of the sentences below. Select the best answer to complete the sentence.

1　" ____ car is this?" "Oh, it's my elder brother's."

　　A　Whose　　B　Whom　　C　Of whose　　D　For who

2　Every winter I enjoy seeing those mountains ____ white snow.

　　A　being covered over　　B　covering with

　　C　covered over　　　　　D　covered with

3　You are gaining weight. You had better ____ your sugar intake.

　　A　cut down up　　B　cut down to　　C　cut down with　　D　cut down on

4　It has been very unusual this year because we have not had ____ snow.

　　A　little　　B　few　　C　less　　D　much

5　The move by G7 nations will prevent any shipments of semi-conductors and natural gas from ____ the country.

　　A　reaching　　B　reach　　C　to be reached　　D　be reaching

Dialog ⑥ 🎧 **19**
Fill in the blanks.
（CD を聴き空白部分を書き取り暗記しましょう。）

［A：post office clerk　B：Japanese traveler］

A：May I help you?

B：I ＿＿＿＿＿ ＿＿＿＿＿ ＿＿＿＿＿ ＿＿＿＿＿ ＿＿＿＿＿ to Japan by air.

A：Let me weigh it first.

B：＿＿＿＿＿ ＿＿＿＿＿ ＿＿＿＿＿ ＿＿＿＿＿?

A：Forty-five dollars.

B：＿＿＿＿＿ ＿＿＿＿＿ ＿＿＿＿＿ ＿＿＿＿＿ ＿＿＿＿＿?

A：About a week.

B：Here's fifty dollars.

A：Out of fifty. ＿＿＿＿＿ ＿＿＿＿＿ ＿＿＿＿＿. Have a nice day.

Promenade 6

米国のノーベル賞受賞者数（2001 年〜2021 年）

全受賞者数	外国生まれ	外国生まれ / 自然科学分野
138	43	33 / 94

アメリカ最古の大学　ハーバード大学

アイビーリーグ（Ivy League）大学
アメリカがイギリスの植民地時代（コーネル大以外）に設立された下記
8大学（設立順）。全て私立大学で北東部にある。
Harvard（1636年設立）, Yale, Princeton, Columbia, Pennsylvania, Brown,
Dartmouth, Cornell（1865年設立）
尚、William & Mary, UC Berkeley, UCLA, Michigan(Ann Arbor), Virginia
等の州立大学を Public Ivy League と呼ぶこともある。

I　Passage 🎧20　　　　　　　　　◆ Words & Phrases

Many American **institutions** and venues take names after their **founders** or donators in their honor. Universities are no exception. In the early 2020s, some media across the globe such as the BBC relied on the data of the **accumulated**
5 **infections** and deaths by COVID-19 by country released by Johns Hopkins University in Baltimore near Washington D.C.

Johns Hopkins University is a private university founded in 1876 as the nation's first research institution. Its founder, Johns Hopkins, was a **philanthropist** and an **entrepreneur**
10 interested in advancing public health and education. Becoming wealthy by succeeding in the wholesale business and the railroad industry, Hopkins donated seven million dollars to build a hospital with a training college, a university and an **orphanage** in Baltimore. Enrolling over 26000 students, the
15 university now has over a dozen schools, centers, and institutes, including the School of Medicine and the School of Public Health. Johns Hopkins University is now one of the most **prestigious** universities, enjoying global fame in medicine. As of 2021, it has produced thirty-nine Nobel laureates.
20 Stanford University near San Francisco in California has also taken its name from its founder. Leland Stanford, a former California Governor, was a successful businessman in the railroad industry. Inspired by his fifteen-year-old son's death from **typhoid** in 1884, he and his wife Jane, in 1885, donated
25 their wealth as well as vast land of over 8000 acres to promote the public welfare. Located amidst **Silicon Valley**, Stanford University has played a key role in creating and developing the IT industry in the region and beyond. Frederick Terman, the Father of Silicon Valley, was one of its **faculty**.
30 Harvard University, the oldest college in America founded in 1636 near Boston, was named after John Harvard. Mr. Harvard, a minister, donated his books and half of his estate to the school to educate local boys to be ministers. **Instruction** has since greatly changed becoming more **secular**. Among the Harvard
35 **alumni** are President John F. Kennedy, President Barack

institutions
機関、大学
founders 創設者

accumulated 累計の
infections 感染者数

philanthropist
慈善家
entrepreneur 実業家

orphanage 孤児院

prestigious 著名な

typhoid 腸チフス

Silicon Valley
ITやハイテク関連企
業が集まる地区

faculty 教官、教授

instruction 授業内容
secular 世俗的な
alumni 卒業生

Obama, and Bill Gates, the founder of *Microsoft*.

Ⅱ Listening Comprehension (21)

Choose the correct answer about the passage.

1   A   near the nation's capital Washington D.C.

   B   near Boston

   C   in the railroad industry

   D   more than ten schools and centers

2   A   Harvard University was founded.

   B   No, it was in 1885.

   C   Stanford's son died.

   D   Hopkins donated 7 million dollars to build a hospital.

3   A   president of an IT company near San Francisco

   B   the first president of Stanford University

   C   a minister

   D   a professor at Stanford University

4   A   It kept releasing the date about COVID-19.

   B   America's first research institution

   C   It played an important role in the IT industry.

   D   strong in medicine

Additional Listening Practice ⑦

Choose the best response to the question or statement.

1   A   B   C

2   A   B   C

Ⅲ　Writing　⑦　現在完了形

Exercise 1 ［　　］内の語 (句) を並べ替え日本文にあう英文を書きなさい。
(注：句読点等は要適宜対応)

1 「アメリカを訪問したことがありますか？」「いいえ、ありません。」

［ever, have, visited, you, haven't, America, no, I］

_____

2 その男優がなくなってから 10 年が過ぎました。

［died, passed, years, the actor, since, have, ten］

_____

3 私は父がくれた時計を失くしてしまった。

［have, me, the watch, I, gave, which, lost, my father］

_____

Exercise 2 次の各日本文にあう英文を**完了形（have/has/had ＋過去分詞）**を使って書いてみましょう。

1 君はその老人が、その大きな家に何年、独りで住んでいるか知っていますか。

→ _____

2 数学の宿題が終わったらサッカーをしに行っても良いよ。

→ _____

3 我々が友人を見送りに空港に着いた時、その飛行機は既に出発していた。

→ _____

Ⅳ　TOEIC® ⑦
Incomplete Sentence → Reading Section の文中下線に入る適語（句）を選ぶ問題に挑戦しよう！

A word or phrase is missing in each of the sentences below. Select the best answer to complete the sentence.

1 ____ what she said, the old man seems to have nothing to do with the accident.

    A　Judging from　　　　B　Judging by

    C　Accordance with　　　D　Accorded to

2 The city of Osaka used to be ____ city in Japan behind Tokyo.

    A　two larger　　　　B　the second largest

    C　the less larger　　D　the second larger

3 No one knows why Susan went out of the room without ____ a word.

    A　to say　　B　not saying　　C　to be saying　　D　saying

4 Since my vocabulary is limited, I am not sure if I can make myself ____ in English.

    A　understand　　B　understanding

    C　understood　　D　to understand

5　It will be hard to hold a concert there because the recovery from the last month's typhoon is not yet ＿＿＿.

　　　A　completed　　　B　completion　　　C　to complete　　　D　completing

V　Dialog ⑦ 🎧 22
Fill in the blanks.
（CD を聴き空白部分を書き取り暗記しましょう。）

［A：visitor　　B：museum staff member　　C：another visitor］

A：Excuse me. Are we allowed to ＿＿＿＿＿＿ ＿＿＿＿＿＿ ＿＿＿＿＿＿?

B：Sure. But no flashes, please.

A：(*After a while*) Excuse me, but will you take a picture of me?

B：＿＿＿＿＿＿ ＿＿＿＿＿＿ ＿＿＿＿＿＿ ＿＿＿＿＿＿. I'm on duty now.

A：Oh, I see. (*To another visitor nearby*) Excuse me.

　　Will you take a picture of me in front of this picture?

C：Sure. But you've got to show me ＿＿＿＿＿＿ ＿＿＿＿＿＿ ＿＿＿＿＿＿

　　＿＿＿＿＿＿ ＿＿＿＿＿＿.

A：Sure. ＿＿＿＿＿＿ ＿＿＿＿＿＿ ＿＿＿＿＿＿ ＿＿＿＿＿＿ ＿＿＿＿＿＿

　　is just press this button here.

C：All right. OK. Smile. (*After taking a picture*) ＿＿＿＿＿＿ ＿＿＿＿＿＿

　　＿＿＿＿＿＿.

Promenade 7

創設者の名前を冠する有名な施設等

☆ **Carnegie Hall（カーネギーホール）**

ニューヨーク市 7 番街、セントラルパークの南にあるコンサートホール。

鉄鋼業で巨万の富を築いた鉄鋼王 Andrew Carnegie（英国スコットランドからの移民 1848）に資金提供を受け 1891 年創設。

また、カーネギーはかつての鉄の街ピッツバーグに Carnegie Mellon University の前身の Carnegie Technical Schools、後の Carnegie Institute of Technology の設立や各地に 2500 以上の図書館設置にも尽力した。

☆ **Rockefeller Center（ロカフェラーセンター）**

ニューヨーク市マンハッタン 5 番街にある複合ビル。

石油産業で巨万の富を築いた John D. Rockefeller により 1930 年に設立。冬場になると同センター前には名物のアイススケートリンクがオープンする（右写真）。

Unit 8　GPA & Studying at American Colleges

アメリカの大学数　約4000（米国教育省）
ほとんどは州立か私立で、その割合はおよそ1対3。学期は
semester制（年間2学期制）か quarter制（年間4学期制）
がほとんどだが、前者が多い。また、夏休み中にサマーセッ
ションの半集中講座を受講して単位取得も可能。

Ⅰ　Passage 23

◆ Words & Phrases

　　Are you interested in studying at an American university?
Each university or college has different **requirements** for
admission. They usually require the **submission** of scores of
tests such as SAT (Scholastic Aptitude Test), and high school
5　**transcripts**. Some require an interview or an essay **describing**
applicants' motives to study at the selected college.
International students from non-English speaking countries are
usually required to **submit** scores of TOEFL-iBT, a test of
English as a foreign language. The score for admission varies
10　from **institution** to institution or the major.

　　Once you are in college, regular attendance and **GPA** (Grade
Point Average) must be students' top **concerns**. Their
academic performance is evaluated on a GPA-4-point scale by
grading A, B, C, D, and F. Scores are given as follows; 4 is given
15　for an A, 3 for a B, 2 for a C, 1 for a D and zero for an F, failure.

　　Skipping classes makes you look bad, which negatively
affects the GPA. To get the most of your college experience,
optimize teachers' office hours, and make use of school
libraries, some of which are open around the clock. At the end
20　of each semester or quarter, students receive a report of
grading and their current GPA. If a student's **cumulative** GPA
does not meet the **criteria** of the university, the student will be
required to perform better to raise their GPA in a year or so.
Some universities may even expel students from the school
25　unless their GPA improves. The higher the GPA is, the better.
This holds true if students want to **transfer** to another college
with a better scholarship or go on to study at a **graduate
school**. GPA also can be a factor in employment.

　　Many American universities provide on-campus residence for
30　students. Students can enjoy **interaction** with other students
from various areas in America as well as with international
students.

　　Unlike Japanese universities, American universities and
colleges do not have **law schools** or medical schools in their
35　undergraduate course. To study law or medicine, American

requirements
入学要件
submission 提出
transcripts
成績証明書
describing 述べた

submit 提出する

institution 大学
GPA 成績評価値
concerns 関心事

optimize 活用する

cumulative 累計の
criteria 基準

transfer 編入する
graduate school
大学院

interaction 交流

law schools
法科大学院

students go on to graduate schools, which **are referred to** as professional schools. Law schools usually provide a three-year course while medical schools a four-year course. Business Schools are another professional school for an **MBA** (Master of Business Administration), which is usually a two-year program.

are referred to~
~と呼ばれる

MBA 経営修士号

Ⅱ Listening Comprehension 24

Choose the correct answer about the passage.

1. A GPA
   B MBA
   C SAT
   D skipping classes

2. A lowering their GPA
   B avoiding libraries
   C visiting teachers during their office hours
   D work around the clock

3. A usually a two-year program
   B a three-year course
   C each semester or quarter
   D at teachers' office hours

4. A in graduate schools
   B in resident housing on campus
   C at law school
   D to get professional experience

Additional Listening Practice ⑧

Listen to two short conversations and choose the best answers for the questions.

1. A Tom's new car   B a parking lot where Tom parks his car
   C Tom doesn't like rain.   D a park nearby the apartment Tom lives in

2. A She will be attending a meeting.   B She forgot her husband's birthday.
   C on Tuesday next week   D She will do some shopping.

Exercise 1 ［　　］内の語（句）を並べ替え日本文にあう英文を書きなさい。
（注：句読点等は要適宜対応）

1 我々全員、その知らせを聞いて非常に喜びました。

［were, the news, all, happy, hear, we, to, very］

_____

2 今朝は始発のバスに乗るために早起きした。

［early, this, to, I, the first, catch, got, morning, up, bus］

_____

3 時々、母は姉に片付け（皿洗い）を手伝うように言います。

［wash, tells, help her, the dishes, sometimes, my sister, our mother, to］

_____

Exercise 2　次の各日本文にあう英文を**不定詞（to ＋動詞の原形）**を使って書いてみましょう。

1 とても危険なので、父は我々にその川では泳がないようにと言っている。

→ _____

2 その試験に合格するのは非常に難しい。先生は我々に毎日勉強するように言っている。

→ _____

3 私はその事故とは無関係です。事故が起こった時、偶然その場にいただけです。

→ _____

Ⅳ **TOEIC®** ⑧

Incomplete Sentence → Reading Section の文中下線に入る適語（句）を選ぶ問題に挑戦しよう！

A word or phrase is missing in each of the sentences below. Select the best answer to complete the sentence.

1 I'm sure you will pass the exam next time if you study ____ .

　　A hardly　　B hard　　C more hard　　D much hardly

2 Our mission here is to help villagers live ____ again as they did before the war.

　　A peaceful　　B in peacefully　　C peacefully　　D in peaceful

3 He's the tallest boy in our class and runs fastest ____ .

　　A of all the boys　　B in all the boys

　　C all in the boys　　D of the all boys

4 "I have to go now. I really enjoyed ____ to you." "Me, too."

　　A talking　　B to talking　　C to be talked　　D to talk

5 Had I known your e-mail address, I ____ you.

　　A could text　　B have texted　　C could have texted　　D texted

Fill in the blanks.
（CD を聴き空白部分を書き取り暗記しましょう。）

［A：store clerk　B：female customer］

A：Good afternoon. May I help you?

B：Yes. I'm ＿＿＿＿＿ ＿＿＿＿＿ ＿＿＿＿＿ ＿＿＿＿＿ for my mother.

A：What kind of gift ＿＿＿＿＿ ＿＿＿＿＿ ＿＿＿＿＿ ＿＿＿＿＿
　　＿＿＿＿＿?

B：I ＿＿＿＿＿ ＿＿＿＿＿ ＿＿＿＿＿. What do you recommend?

A：How about some perfume?

B：＿＿＿＿＿ ＿＿＿＿＿. It smells nice. How much is it?

A：$35, plus tax.

B：Fine. ＿＿＿＿＿ ＿＿＿＿＿ ＿＿＿＿＿. Here's 50 dollars.

A：I'll be ＿＿＿＿＿ ＿＿＿＿＿ ＿＿＿＿＿ ＿＿＿＿＿ ＿＿＿＿＿.

Promenade 8

多くのアメリカの大学キャンパスで目を引くのは、木々と芝生の緑の
多さ。また、その木々の中や芝生の上で戯れる栗鼠（りす）の多さ。
読書や勉強で疲れた時、そんなかわいい栗鼠の戯れが一時の癒しを提
供してくれる。

Unit 9 Los Angeles - A Center of Entertainment

ロサンゼルス
ニューヨークに次ぐアメリカ第二の都市。
市のみの人口は 400 万人程だが、広域の都市圏は
約 1400 万人。サンベルト地帯に位置し気候も温暖
で人や行事を惹きつける。

I Passage 〔26〕   ◆ Words & Phrases

　Pay attention to the spelling of the Los *Angeles* Angels, an American professional baseball team. *Angels* is English while *angeles* is Spanish, which implies the city's ties with Spain. Los Angeles, often **referred to** as L.A., was once a town under
5 Spanish rule amid a desert in southern California. Although Mexico later took it over, it remained only a town after America took over California in 1848. As of 2022, L.A., the nation's busiest port, is the second largest city with about four million people.

10 　Los Angeles, in development, fell behind San Francisco, another major city in California. While the discovery of gold in the late 1840s contributed to the growth of San Francisco, L.A. owed its growth to the discovery of oil and natural gas in the 1890s. L. A. soon became the nation's oil production center.

15 　L.A.'s growth gained **momentum** after the turn of the century. A developing water supply **launched** in 1908 provided water to homes and farms, helping the area grow and expand. L.A. drew more global attention as a center of entertainment. In 1910, Los Angeles **merged** with the **adjacent** city of Hollywood,
20 **prospering** with a movie industry of ten film corporations. Developing another face with its film industry, L.A.'s population reached one million in 1930. The Los Angeles metropolitan area raised its **name recognition** further with the opening of theme parks such as Disneyland in Anaheim in 1955 and Universal
25 Studios in Hollywood in 1964. L.A. has hosted major annual American entertainment awards ceremonies, such as the Academy Awards for **film achievements** at Hollywood's Dolby Theatre and the Grammy Awards for music achievements. The greater Hollywood area including Beverly Hills and Los Feriz is
30 home to celebrities, such as Taylor Swift, Madonna, Angelina Jolie, Leonardo DiCaprio, and Brad Pitt.

　Los Angeles has a common face with other major U.S. cities. One is ethnic diversity. As of 2020, 47 percent of its population was Hispanic, 29% White, 12% Asian and 8% Afro-American.
35 Granted that L.A. has serious problems, such as gun or drug

referred to
〜と呼ばれる

momentum 勢い
launch 始める

merge 合併する
adjacent 隣の
prosper 繁栄する

name recognition
知名度

film achievements
（制作）映画の功績

related crimes, rising **robberies** and homelessness, the city
continues to grow, hosting its third Olympic Games in 2028.

robberies
強盗や盗難事件

Ⅱ　Listening Comprehension ⓐ27

Choose the correct answer about the passage.

1　A　47% was Hispanic.

　　B　over one million

　　C　No, it was in 1892.

　　D　L.A. became the second largest city in America.

2　A　Disneyland opened.

　　B　Hollywood joined the city of Los Angeles.

　　C　Oil was discovered near L.A.

　　D　Brad Pitt moved to Beverly Hills.

3　A　Mexico

　　B　America in 1848

　　C　Spain did.

　　D　Yes, Mexico took it from Spain.

4　A　More Asian-Americans live in L.A. than Blacks or Afro-Americans.

　　B　L.A. developed earlier than San Francisco.

　　C　L.A. has no problem with homelessness.

　　D　Many celebrities used to live in Hollywood.

Additional Listening Practice　⑨

Choose the best response to the question or statement.

1　A　　　B　　　C

2　A　　　B　　　C

Writing ⑨ **比較**1

Exercise 1 〔　　〕内の語（句）を並べ替え日本文にあう英文を書きなさい。
（注：句読点等は要適宜対応）

1　今年の夏は去年より涼しい。　　　〔is, than, summer, last, this, cooler, year〕

_____

2　これは、この美術館で一番古い絵です。

〔picture, is, this museum, oldest, this, in, the〕

_____

3　スポーツの中で何が一番好きですか。〔of, do, sport, all, like, you, which, best〕

_____

Exercise 2　次の各日本文にあう英文を**比較表現**に注意して書いてみましょう。

1　日本語は中国語より難しいと言う人もいるが、僕はそうは思わない。

→ _____

2　次郎は祖父より早く起きる。実は、彼は我が家で一番早く起きる。

〔実は ☞ as a matter of fact〕

→ _____

3　春になって日がだんだん長くなっている。僕は季節の中で春が一番好きだ。

→ _____

Ⅳ　**TOEIC**® ⑨
Incomplete Sentence → Reading Section の文中下線に入る適語（句）を選ぶ問題に挑戦しよう！

A word or phrase is missing in each of the sentences below. Select the best answer to complete the sentence.

1　"How soon do you think he will return?" "I am not sure, but I think he will come back ____ three at latest."

　　　A　by　　B　until　　C　to　　D　till

2　No one in our class was able to answer when and where Abraham Lincoln ____ .

　　　A　born　　B　being born　　C　was bore　　D　was born

3　Many VIPs are arriving at the newly-opened airport to ____ the meeting held in the city.

　　　A　attend to　　B　attend　　C　attending at　　D　attend at

4　The letter said that my host family, ____ I spent last summer, had moved into a new house.

　　　A　with whom　　B　whom　　C　who　　D　where

5　Many language teachers agree that practice makes perfect in learning any foreign language and ____.

　　　A　so it does　　B　so does it　　C　so it is　　D　so is it

Fill in the blanks.
（CD を聴き空白部分を書き取り暗記しましょう。）

［A：hotel staff member　B：guest］

A：Good morning, sir.

B：I ＿＿＿＿＿＿ ＿＿＿＿＿＿ ＿＿＿＿＿＿ ＿＿＿＿＿＿.

A：All right. I'll get your bill ready.

B：＿＿＿＿＿＿ ＿＿＿＿＿＿ ＿＿＿＿＿＿ ＿＿＿＿＿＿ ＿＿＿＿＿＿
＿＿＿＿＿＿ to the airport?

A：From right ＿＿＿＿＿＿ ＿＿＿＿＿＿ ＿＿＿＿＿＿, in front of the Marriott
Hotel.

B：Thank you.

A：＿＿＿＿＿＿ ＿＿＿＿＿＿ ＿＿＿＿＿＿ ＿＿＿＿＿＿.

Promenade 9

ロサンゼルスが娯楽エンターテインメントの中心である一つの指標

☆映画の祭典アカデミー賞の授与式が開催された都市と回数

　初回から今日までロサンゼルスかその近郊

　＊1961-68年　ロサンゼルス市隣のサンタモニカ市

☆音楽の祭典グラミー賞の授与式が開催された都市と回数

　　ロサンゼルス-51回

　　ニューヨーク-22回

　　他 7回

　＊2000年以降は2003年（ニューヨーク）、2022年（ラスベガス）以外は
　　ロサンゼルスで開催。

@Dmileson

1872 年、アメリカ初の映画が制作されたといわれる。
ただ、1910 年代頃までは無声映画だった。1929 年アカデミー賞
が創設され映画への関心が高まり、1930 年代、米国人の 65％が
週 1 の頻度で映画鑑賞し映画は完全に娯楽化した。1940 年代、
カラー映像と音質両面の向上で映画鑑賞者数は急増し、戦後、ハ
リウッドは「黄金時代」を迎えることになった。

I Passage 29

◆ Words & Phrases

　　In early 1910, a filmmaking party led by **director** D.W.
Griffith reached downtown Los Angeles. The group was sent
there by the Biograph Company, a motion picture firm in New
York. The party before long moved ten miles north to a little
5　village where they found friendly residents who liked to see
them make films. They also liked the sunny weather, mild
climate, and the open lot for varied film settings ideal for
filmmaking throughout the year. The name of the place was
Hollywood. After making some films, they returned to New
10　York with good news of Hollywood. **Lured** by the news, several
aspiring filmmakers, such as Universal and Warner Bros.,
moved their studios to Hollywood years later. **Merging** with
Los Angeles in 1910, Hollywood **burgeoned** into a center of
film production, making it a **synonym** of the film industry.

15　　**Flourishing** with producing films, Hollywood produced
movie stars. In 1927, **the Academy of Motion Picture Arts
and Sciences** was founded in Beverly Hills to recognize
achievement in the film industry. At the Hollywood Roosevelt
Hotel in 1929, the Academy held a party to present awards for
20　excellent films, directors, actors, and others in 12 categories,
the start of the Academy Awards, also known as the Oscars.
Hollywood has since hosted the ceremony held in spring. In the
last 20 years, the Dolby Theatre, **formerly**-the Kodak Theatre,
has served as the presentation's **venue** where red carpets
25　welcome the nominees. Winners receive the gold-plate
statuette, the Oscar. The Awards was first televised in America
in 1953 and globally in 1969, winning more audience and fame.
The Oscars now enjoy the highest **prestige** in the
entertainment industry.

30　　The Academy's prestige never came without reform. They
created the awards such as the Best International Feature Film
for non-English films in 1947 and the Best Animated Feature
Film for animated films in 2001. The Japanese movies *Drive My
Car* won the former award in 2021 and ***Spirited Away*** by
35　Hayao Miyazaki did the latter in 2002. The Oscars are now

director 映画監督

lured 魅了されて
aspiring 野心のある
merge 合併する
burgeon 発展する
synonym 同義語
flourish 繁栄する
**the Academy of
Motion Picture Arts
and Sciences** 映画芸
術科学アカデミー
achievement 功績

formerly かつて
venue 会場

statuette 像

prestige 名声
**entertainment
industry** 娯楽産業

Spirited Away
「千と千尋の神隠し」

awarded in over twenty categories, such as Best Picture, Best Actor, and Best Director. Among the famous films that received the award for Best Picture are *Gone with the Wind* in 1939, *The Sound of Music* in 1965 and *Titanic* in 1997, to name a few.

II   Listening Comprehension 🎧 30

Choose the correct answer about the passage.

1 A at the Hollywood Roosevelt Hotel
  B A party was held at a hotel.
  C The ceremony was first televised abroad.
  D *Gone with the Wind* won the award.

2 A in twelve categories
  B in the last twenty years
  C at the Dolby Theatre in Hollywood
  D ever since 1929

3 A in 1997
  B D.W. Griffith did.
  C A few actors did.
  D   not clear from the passage

4 A Hollywood was not part of Los Angeles first.
  B *The Sound of Music* is an animated film.
  C The climate in Hollywood suited filmmaking.
  D The number of awards has changed.

Additional Listening Practice   ⑩

Listen to two short conversations and choose the best answers for the questions.

1 A Mr. White was.   B Makoto and Mr. White are.
  C Mr. White is.   D Cathy is.

2 A He'll wait for the next airport bus.
  B He'll walk to the nearest subway station.
  C He'll call the airline company.
  D He won't take the subway.

III　Writing　⑩　比較 2

Exercise 1　［　　］内の語（句）を並べ替え日本文にあう英文を書きなさい。
（注：句読点等は要適宜対応）

1　この新しい橋は古い橋より幅が広くて長い。
　　　　　　　　　　［wider, new, is, one, than, and, this, bridge, longer, the old］
　_____

2　ヒロシはそのバスケットボールチームで 2 番目に背が高い男の子だ。
　　　　　　　　［is, the basketball, on, boy, tallest, team, Hiroshi, the second］
　_____

3　私には兄が一人います。彼は私より 3 歳年上です。（2 文に分けて）
　　　　　　　［senior, older brother, me, three years, one, he, I, is, have, to］
　_____

Exercise 2　次の各日本文にあう英文を**比較表現**に注意して書いてみましょう。

1　「君はお茶とコーヒーではどちらが好きですか。」「お茶よりもコーヒーが好きです。」
　→ _____

2　東京スカイツリーは世界で一番高い塔です。それは東京タワーの約 2 倍の高さです。　　　　　　　　　　　　　　　　　　　　　　　　　　　　　［塔 ☞ tower］
　→ _____

3　練習をすればするほど、その楽器をより上手くひけるようになるよ。
　→ _____

IV　TOEIC® ⑩

Incomplete Sentence → Reading Section の文中下線に入る適語（句）を選ぶ問題に挑戦しよう！

A word or phrase is missing in each of the sentences below. Select the best answer to complete the sentence.

1　Some doctors have been very much concerned about how the new vaccine ____ the human body.

　　A　effects　　B　have affect　　C　affects　　D　was affected

2　It is this company's policy to determine the starting salary ____ your age and previous career.

　　A　depend on　　　　B　to be dependent on
　　C　depending on　　　D　being depend on

3　____ are you as well as your son signing up for this elementary course for?

　　A　Why　　B　What　　C　When　　D　How

4　Hardly ＿＿＿ the dinner for the party when some guests started arriving.

  A　I had prepared   B　had I preparing

  C　had I been prepared D　had I prepared

5　Each one of us ＿＿＿ an assignment every week, usually a written report to be handed in on Mondays.

  A　were given B　was given C　gave D　have given

Ⅴ　Dialog ⑩ 31

Fill in the blanks.

（CD を聴き空白部分を書き取り暗記しましょう。）

[A：airline staff member　B：passenger]

A：Hi! May I help you?

B：Yes. ＿＿＿＿＿＿ ＿＿＿＿＿＿ ＿＿＿＿＿＿ ＿＿＿＿＿＿ ＿＿＿＿＿＿.

A：All right. ＿＿＿＿＿＿ ＿＿＿＿＿＿ ＿＿＿＿＿＿ ＿＿＿＿＿＿, please.

B：＿＿＿＿＿＿ ＿＿＿＿＿＿ ＿＿＿＿＿＿.

A：＿＿＿＿＿＿ ＿＿＿＿＿＿ ＿＿＿＿＿＿ ＿＿＿＿＿＿ ＿＿＿＿＿＿

 ＿＿＿＿＿＿?

B：Two. But I want to keep this small bag with me.

A：＿＿＿＿＿＿. Window or aisle seat?

B：Window, please.

A：Okay. All set. Here's your boarding pass. ＿＿＿＿＿＿ ＿＿＿＿＿＿

 ＿＿＿＿＿＿ ＿＿＿＿＿＿.

Promenade 10

アカデミー賞授与式は毎年 2 月末か 3 月初旬の日曜日に開催される。会場にはリムジンで到着する各賞・部門の候補者（nominee）も少なくない。

受賞の対象になるには一定の条件がある。例えば、前年度に上映開始され、ロサンゼルス郡内の映画館で、ある一定期間上映された映画であることなど。ただ、各賞によってルールが異なるようである。

Unit 11　Abortion-Pro-Choice vs. Pro-Life

連邦最高裁判所。判事数 9 名で任期は終身

アメリカで人工妊娠中絶の是非についての論争が再燃している。
PRO-CHOICE（妊娠中絶容認）vs. PRO-LIFE（妊娠中絶反対）
妊娠中絶（abortion）への米国人の考え方の世論調査
・70%……女性と医師に判断をゆだねるべき。
・58%……全て、又は多くの場合、認めるべき。
（米国 ABC テレビとワシントンポスト紙／2022 年 4 月）
＊ Gallup 調査では中絶容認派が 85%に達した。（同年 5 月）

I　Passage 🎧 32　　　　　　　　　◆ Words & Phrases

　　American society is divided on **abortion**. In June 2022, **the U.S. Supreme Court** in a 5-4 decision **overturned** the half a century old **Roe v. Wade decision**^注 made in 1973. The 1973 decision had made abortion **legal** nationwide as a right
5　guaranteed under **the U.S. Constitution**. Now the new decision would **deprive** women of their rights to abortion, making it **state politicians** not women who decide what they can do with their bodies. As of summer 2022, over a dozen states such as California, Oregon, and New York legally protect
10　the right to abortion. More than a dozen states such as Texas, Oklahoma, and Kentucky **ban** or severely limit abortion. Texas and Oklahoma allow abortion in the case of medical **emergencies**, but not to the victims of rape and **incest**. Women in these states would have to cross state lines for abortion. After
15　the decision, corporate giants such as Starbucks, Disney, Apple, Microsoft, Uber and more expressed their intentions to cover travel costs for their employees seeking out-of-state abortions. The new decision changed the American landscape.

　　Abortion supporters, who criticized the new decision, have
20　long held the slogan of PRO-CHOICE. They **argue** that abortion is a personal matter and part of women's right to choose. President Joe Biden joined them, calling the new decision 'a tragic error'. Biden commented, "It's a sad day for the Court and the nation. Fifty years ago, Roe v. Wade was
25　decided and has been the law of the land since then. This **landmark** case protected a woman's right to choose, free from political **interference**."

　　Those against abortion with the slogan of PRO-LIFE welcomed the new decision. They argue that abortion is
30　nothing but killing. Former President Donald Trump gave himself credit, calling the new decision "the biggest win for life in a generation". Trump **nominated** three **conservative justices** to the Supreme Court made of nine justices while in office. All three joined to overturn the 1973 decision.

35　　Many Americans are PRO-CHOICE. Both NBC News and

◆ Words & Phrases

abortion 妊娠中絶
the U.S. Supreme Court 連邦最高裁判所
overturn 覆す
legal 合法
the U.S. Constitution 合衆国憲法
deprive 奪う
state politicians 州の政治家

ban 禁止する

emergencies（母体に危険が及ぶ）緊急事態
incest 近親相姦

argue 主張する

landmark 画期的な
interference 介入

nominate 指名する
conservative justices 保守的な判事

NPR/PBS NewsHour found in their **polls** in May nearly two-thirds of Americans support abortion. What is called for now is how **state and federal** lawmakers will respond to this, their commitment to protection of the basic human right.

NPR 米国公共ラジオ
PBS 米国公共テレビ
polls 世論調査
state and federal
州と国の

注：Roe v. Wade decision 人工妊娠中絶を規制するテキサス州法を 7 対 2 で
　　合衆国憲法違反とし中絶を女性の権利とした判決。

Ⅱ　Listening Comprehension 〔33〕

Choose the correct answer about the passage.

1　A　President Trump supported it.

　　B　It protected abortion as women's right.

　　C　Pro-Life supporters' slogan.

　　D　Yes, Oregon protects the right to abortion.

2　A　nine

　　B　in 2016

　　C　three

　　D　No, it was President Joe Biden.

3　A　Oklahoma, too.

　　B　Yes, it is.

　　C　Only in the case of saving the mother's life.

　　D　Some state politicians in Texas do.

4　A　The U.S. Supreme Court has nine justices.

　　B　Three new justices seem to be Pro-Life supporters.

　　C　Some companies such as Disney are for abortion.

　　D　President Biden welcomed the 2022 decision.

Additional Listening Practice　⑪

Choose the best response to the question or statement.

1　A　　　B　　　C

2　A　　　B　　　C

Ⅲ　Writing　⑪　関係代名詞

Exercise 1　[　　　]内の語（句）を並べ替え日本文にあう英文を書きなさい。
（注：文字サイズ、句読点は要適宜対応）

1　私には英語が得意な友人がいる。[have, good, a friend, I, is, at, English, who]

_____

2　君が昨日、買った新しいパソコンを見せてくれ。

[you, new, me, the, PC, yesterday, bought, which, show]

_____

3　昨夜、君がテレビで見た歌手がテイラー・スウィフトだよ。

[on, singer, is, whom, saw, night, Taylor Swift, TV, the, last, you]

_____

Exercise 2　次の各日本文にあう英文を**関係代名詞（who, which, what 等）**を使って書いてみましょう。

1　先々月、父が買った新車は、とても燃費が良い。　[燃費が良い ☞ fuel-efficient]
→ _____

2　その警官は、その黒い帽子をかぶった不審者にバッグの中（に持っている物）を見せるように言った。
　　→ _____

3　君がそこで会った方が我々の新しい英語の先生だ。彼について私が知っていることを君に話しておく。
　　→ _____

Ⅳ　TOEIC® ⑪
Incomplete Sentence → Reading Section の文中下線に入る適語（句）を選ぶ問題に挑戦しよう！

A word or phrase is missing in each of the sentences below. Select the best answer to complete the sentence.

1　Of late, women rent *kimonos* for special occasions because renting one is ＿＿＿ than buying one.

A　a lot of cheaper　B　a lot cheaper　C　more cheap　D　much cheap

2　My host family advised me ＿＿＿ to the park for jogging after dark.

A　to not go　B　to go not　C　not to go　D　do not go

3　The couple was having ＿＿＿ at the party that they were unaware that it was almost midnight.

A　so a good time　B　such good a time

C　very a good time　D　such a good time

4 The flood is reported to _____ the nation's farm land so badly that it is causing a
   food shortage.

  A has damaged B having damaged C have damaged D damaged

5 I missed the last bus again. I _____ the office earlier.

  A had left B could leave C should have left D can have left

V Dialog ⑪ 🎧 34
Fill in the blanks.
（CD を聴き空白部分を書き取り暗記しましょう。）

[A：foreigner B：Japanese]

A：Excuse me. _____ _____ _____ _____?

B：Yes, a little. _____ _____ _____ _____?

A：Yes, where's the nearest post office?

B：It's the white building _____ _____ _____ _____.

A：Oh, _____ _____ _____ _____.

B：Don't mention it.

Promenade 11

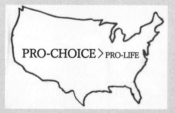

PRO-CHOICE > PRO-LIFE

トランプ政権誕生以降からか、アメリカ社会の"分断"が顕在化してきた。多発する銃犯罪への銃規制、不法移民対策、白人警官らによる黒人殺害、過剰取り締まりに見る人種差別。そして今回の連邦最高裁判所の歴史的判決で再燃した人工妊娠中絶是非論争。いずれもアメリカの古くて新しい問題である。

半世紀前の連邦最高裁判所の判決を覆した今回の同最高裁判所の判決の影響は大きい。この判決と前後してニュースになった6月、中絶を禁止するオハイオ州でレイプの犠牲になった10歳の女児が、中絶のため隣州インディアナ州に行かねばならなかった事案は、中絶是非論争を一層高めることになった。

また、州境を越えて中絶手術をする社員の旅費を負担すること等を表明した企業は、本文に登場した企業以外には次のような企業があった。業種、地域を問わず多くの大企業が名を連ねる。今回の連邦最高裁判決を直接は批判しないものの、中絶を女性の権利として擁護、支援する姿勢を打ち出したもので、アメリカが PRO-CHOICE 社会であることを示している。

Warner Bros., Discovery, CNN, New York Times, Master Card, Yahoo, Target, Meta, Netflix, Accenture, Intel, Alaska Airlines, American Airlines, Bank of America, Match Group, Levi Strauss, JPMorgan Chase, Goldman Sachs, Johnson & Johnson 他

第 16 代大統領
エイブラハム・リンカーン

黒人初の大統領
バラク・オバマ

アフリカ系アメリカ人（黒人）
多民族国家アメリカ社会の中でアフリカ系アメリカ人である黒人
人口は 2020 年時点で約 4100 万人。全人口の約 12.4％を占めまし
た。その皮膚の色だけで差別や不正義の対象になってきた歴史が
ある。

I Passage 🎧35　　　　　　　　　　　◆ Words & Phrases

　　Naomi Osaka, a professional tennis player, played seven matches in the U.S. Open tournament in New York in 2020. In each game, Osaka appeared on the court wearing a different black mask, each of which had the names of seven black

5　**victims** killed by police or non-black **brutality**. One of the names was George Floyd who was killed by a white police officer in Minneapolis in May 2020.The tennis tournament was held amid the COVID-19 pandemic as well as the *Black Lives Matter* (BLM) movement. Naomi helped raise **awareness** of

10　**racism** against African-Americans at home and abroad.

victim 犠牲者
brutality 虐待

awareness 意識
racism 人種差別

　　The year of 1619 was historic in American history. A Dutch ship with twenty Blacks stopped by at the Virginia **colony** built by Great Britain in 1607 on the current east coast. Blacks were traded for food. They were treated as **slaves**. **Slavery** would

15　spread in **the South**. It remained despite **the Declaration of Independence** adopted in 1776 which said that *all men were created equal*. Slavery legally ended in 1865 after President Abraham Lincoln freed Blacks from slavery in 1863 amid **the Civil War**.

colony 植民地

slaves/slavery
奴隷／奴隷制
the South 南部
the Declaration of
Independence
独立宣言
the Civil War
南北戦争　P.7 参照

20　The end of slavery was the start of **blatant** racism against Afro-Americans for a century to come. Especially in the South, they were **discriminated** against in various areas, such as voting rights, access to public facilities like schools, hospitals, hotels, restaurants, and buses. In 1954, the U.S. Supreme Court

25　judged that **segregation** was **unconstitutional** and needed to be mended. The decision led Martin Luther King Jr. and other Black activists to fight for **desegregation**. In the mid 1960s, Blacks won **civil rights** that provided them with equal rights in voting, education, public **accommodations** and some federal

30　programs.

blatant 露骨な

discriminate
〜を差別する

segregation
人種分離・差別
unconstitutional
憲法違反
desegregation
人種差別撤廃
civil rights 公民権
accommodations
施設

　　The civil rights movement has since made significant progress. In 1989, Virginia elected the nation's first Black **governor** Douglas Wilder and in 2009, Barack Obama was elected the first Black president. In 2022, Ketanji Brown

35　Jackson (KBJ) became the first female Black judge to serve on

governor 知事

the Supreme Court. The civil rights movement has come a long way but it has a long way to go yet. KBJ and the BLM movement show it well.

Ⅱ Listening Comprehension 🎧 36

Choose the correct answer about the passage.

1 A No, it was in Minneapolis.

  B a great progress in civil rights

  C the U.S. Open Tennis tournament

  D Seven Black citizens were killed by police brutality.

2 A in 1863

  B The year 1619 was historic.

  C It was in 2022.

  D in the middle of the 1960s

3 A in Virginia

  B the first U.S. elected Black governor

  C in 1989

  D one of the leading Black activists

4 A The slavery ended in 1789.

  B Martin Luther King Jr. was a Black activist.

  C Slavery lasted over two centuries.

  D George Floyd is one of the victims by police brutality.

Additional Listening Practice ⑫

Listen to two short conversations and choose the best answers for the questions.

1 A in a shop   B major credit cards

  C It is six forty-five.   D by card

2 A He is attending a meeting.   B He read a message.

  C He will leave his office before five.   D He will call Mr. Sato.

III Writing ⑫ 形容詞と副詞

Exercise 1 [   ]内の語（句）を並べ替え日本文にあう英文を書きなさい。
（注：句読点等は要適宜対応）

1 彼女は、いつもその新しいスーパーで買い物をします。

[always, her, at, she, the new, does, supermarket, shopping]

_____

2 私の姉は、数年ロンドンで過ごしたので英語を上手に話す。

[speaks, in London, years, well, spent, my sister, some, English, and]

_____

3 ご親切に最寄りの駅までの道を教えていただきありがとうございます。

[the, station, you, nearest, is, to, me, show, it, the way, kind, to, of]

_____

Exercise 2 次の各日本文にあう英文を**形容詞と副詞**に注意して書いてみましょう。

1 私の祖母は派手な服を着るのが好きで、とても若く見える。[派手な ☞ colorful]

→ _____

2 その講演はとてもつまらなくて私は途中眠ってしまった。

→ _____

3 この辺りは普段、早朝は、あまり交通量はない。

→ _____

IV TOEIC® ⑫
Incomplete Sentence → Reading Section の文中下線に入る適語（句）を選ぶ問題に挑戦しよう！

A word or phrase is missing in each of the sentences below. Select the best answer to complete the sentence.

1 The police said that the number of deaths in the train accident had ____ to more than 200.

A rose   B raised   C risen   D to rise

2 I wonder if our son is doing fine because we have not heard from him ____.

A since two months   B during two months

C while two months   D for two months

3 When it comes ____, you can hardly beat him. He won three gold medals in the last Olympics.

A to swimming   B to swim   C swimming   D about swimming

4 The old man told me that he ____ in the park every morning.

A took a walk   B takes a walk

C will take a walk   D was taken a walk

5 The young man said that he had seen the man arguing that night with his neighbor, _____ I believe is a lie.

    A that   B which   C whom   D in which

Ⅴ Dialog ⑫ 🎧 ③⑦
Fill in the blanks.
（CD を聴き空白部分を書き取り暗記しましょう。）

［A：traveler B：Japanese］

A：Excuse me. Do you speak English?

B：Yes, some. _____ _____ _____ _____

    _____?

A：Yes, how can I get to the airport?

B：_____ _____ _____.

A：_____ _____ _____ _____ _____?

B：Two hundred and fifty yen, I think.

A：And _____ _____ _____ _____ _____?

B：About fifteen minutes.

A：Thank you so much.

B：_____ _____ _____.

Promenade 12
Affirmative Action（積極的差別撤廃・改善措置）

1960 年代の公民権運動の成果の一つ。特に黒人を中心に少数民族などに機会均等が保証されなかった過去の差別への償いと、その後の社会的な向上のための施策として導入され現在まで続いている。

具体的には、女性や黒人、アジア系、先住民等の少数民族が大学への入学や雇用時にその割合を増やすために優遇される。

しかし、近年は白人を中心に「逆差別」との批判の声が聞かれるようになってきている。公民権運動は一つの転換期、時代の岐路に立たされている。

Unit 13 Personal Justice Denied -Japanese Americans during WW Ⅱ

第二次世界大戦時の日系アメリカ人の強制収容
戦争が招いた不正義、悲劇、歴史的汚点。それを猛省し謝罪し賠償したアメリカ。
写真左：指定場所に集合した日系人。
　　　　この後、収容所に移送された。
右地図：収容所の地図。Tule Lake（左中）、Manzanar（左下）が見てとれる。

Ⅰ Passage 38 ◆ Words & Phrases

　　Japan and America currently enjoy very **solid** relationships politically, economically, culturally, and militarily. For both nations, however, the first half of the 1940s was the darkest era in their history. World War II did so much damage to both nations.

5　　The era was also a tragic era for the Japanese-Americans living on the West Coast. They were not equally treated like other enemy ethnic groups, German-Americans and Italian-Americans. In May 1942, about 120,000 Japanese-Americans on
10　the West Coast were ordered by the military to give up their residences and report to the designated assembly centers. They were sent to ten **internment camps** mainly in the Rocky Mountains. They had no freedom to leave the camps. Removal of the Japanese-Americans from the West Coast lasted until
15　August 1942.

　　It was Fred T. Korematsu who challenged such **injustice**. Korematsu, 21 years old then, was a second generation Japanese-American living near San Francisco. He did not want to part from his white American girlfriend and did not follow the
20　military order. On May 30, 1942, he was caught, put in jail and **convicted**. He was later **detained** in the relocation camp in Topaz, Utah. Later he took the case to the Supreme Court. On December 18, 1944, the Court supported the military order and his **conviction**.

25　　It took several decades for justice to be done. In 1976, President Gerald Ford admitted that the order was **racist** against the Japanese and officially **apologized**. **The U.S. Congress** also concluded in its 1982 report titled '*Personal Justice Denied*' that the order was based on **racism** against the
30　Japanese, war time hysteria and the lack of political leadership. In 1983, the **federal court overturned** the Korematsu conviction. Also in 1988, Congress expressed regret, which led to the U.S. government's **reparations** of $20,000 for each survivor. It showed its **pledge** to strengthen the good U.S.-
35　Japanese relationship further as well as to make American

solid 堅固な

internment camps 収容所

injustice 不正義

convicted 有罪に
detain 収容する

conviction 有罪

racism/racist
人種差別／的
apologize 謝罪する
the U.S. Congress
アメリカ議会

federal court
連邦裁判所
overturn 覆す
reparations 賠償
pledge 誓い

society more **racism-free**.

racism-free
人種差別のない

Choose the correct answer about the passage.

1 A more than ten in the mountains

   B by the military

   C about 120,000

   D on the West Coast

2 A He reported himself to the assembly center.

   B He was living near San Francisco.

   C He had a white American girlfriend.

   D He was born in America.

3 A President Gerald Ford apologized.

   B The U.S. Congress issued a report.

   C The U.S. top court supported the military order.

   D Korematsu received $20.000 as reparation.

4 A few German-Americans on the West Coast

   B not enough camps

   C Because they were not the enemy aliens.

   D It is not clear from the passage.

Additional Listening Practice ⑬

Choose the best response to the question or statement.

1 A   B   C

2 A   B   C

Exercise 1 ［　　　］内の語（句）を並べ替え日本文にあう英文を書きなさい。
（注：句読点等は要適宜対応）

1 先月、父が僕に中古車を買ってくれた。

[month, me, a, my father, car, bought, last, used]

_____

2 赤い帽子をかぶった婦人は私の叔母です。

[my, the, red, is, hat, aunt, wearing, the lady]

_____

3 うちの娘は妻と買い物に行くのがとても好きです。

[with, of, is, my wife, going, our daughter, very, shopping, fond]

_____

Exercise 2 次の各日本文にあう英文を**分詞（動詞＋ing か過去分詞）**と動名詞（動詞＋ing）に注意して書きなさい。

1 同僚からの電話の後、彼は一言も言わずに部屋を去っていった。

[同僚 ☞ colleague]

→ _____

2 待合室はとても騒がしかったので、弟は名前が呼ばれたのに気付か（聞こえ）なかった。　　　[待合室 ☞ a waiting room]

→ _____

3 次の角を右に曲がると、約300年前に建てられたお寺が見えます。

[〜に曲がると ☞ turning to 〜]

→ _____

Ⅳ TOEIC® ⑬
Incomplete Sentence → Reading Section の文中下線に入る適語（句）を選ぶ問題に挑戦しよう！

A word or phrase is missing in each of the sentences below. Select the best answer to complete the sentence.

1 According to the evening news, the police are still looking for the ____.

    A suspicion　　B suspense　　C suspicious　　D suspect

2 You haven't changed much ____ we met at the farewell party ten years ago.

    A from　　B since　　C when　　D because

3 The man ____ you saw at the train station yesterday is our new English teacher from Canada.

    A whose　　B whom　　C with whom　　D who

4 He was seriously injured by the traffic accident. He ＿＿＿ to live in a wheelchair ever since.

      A has forced   B has been forced

      C had been forcing   D was being forcing

5 I can hardly wait for the ＿＿＿ issue of the magazine. It'll have an article about our company.

      A latest   B late   C last   D latter

V   **Dialog** ⑬

Fill in the blanks.

（CD を聴き空白部分を書き取り暗記しましょう。）

[A：Japanese B：American]

A：May I ask you a question?

B：＿＿＿＿＿＿.＿＿＿＿＿＿＿＿＿＿＿＿.

A：＿＿＿＿＿＿＿＿＿＿＿＿＿＿＿＿＿＿＿＿＿＿＿＿＿＿＿＿ "**PETTO BOTORU**" in English?

B：We say "plastic bottle."

A：Thanks a lot.

B：＿＿＿＿＿＿＿.

Promenade 13

Norman Mineta（1931/11/2-2022/5/3）

Personal Justice Denied

REPORT OF THE COMMISSION ON WARTIME RELOCATION AND INTERNMENT OF CIVILIANS

日系アメリカ人の強制収容連邦議会委員会報告書の表紙。
報告書は 300 頁以上に及ぶ。

第二次世界大戦中に強制収容所に収容された日系アメリカ人で収容所から解放され政治家としてアメリカに貢献した一人。

アメリカ加州サンノゼ生まれ。1942 年、ワイオミング州ハートマウンテン収容所（収容可能数 12000 人）に数年間収容された。

30 代半ばからは政界に入り、地元や連邦議会議員、更には民主、共和の両方の政権の閣僚になり母国アメリカのために尽力した。

・サンノゼ市市会議員（1967-1971）、同市市長（1971-1975）

・連邦議会下院議員（民主、1975-1995）

・商務長官（2000 年、クリントン政権―民主）

・運輸長官（2001 年、ブッシュ政権―共和）

Unit 14 The Hispanics

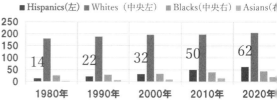

米国人種／民族別人口推移（単位100万人）

■Hispanics(左) ■Whites（中央左） ■Blacks(中央右) ■Asians(右

250
200
150
100
50
0

14　　22　　32　　50　　62

1980年　1990年　2000年　2010年　2020年

出典 US Census 他

ヒスパニック

アメリカでは過去数十年間、ヒスパニック系人口の増加
が著しい。白人が圧倒的に多くを占め、黒人やアジア系
とその他の少数民族で成り立っていた米国のイメージ
は、今は昔になりつつあるようです。

I　Passage 41　　　　　　　　　　◆ Words & Phrases

　　Whites in America are the majority now but may no longer be
in the near future. In 2020, the U.S. population was about 330
million with Whites **composing** 58%, Hispanics 19%, Blacks
13%, and Asians 6%. What is so remarkable is the sharp rise in
5　the Hispanic population. It increased over four times the
number in 1980 when the term Hispanics was first
implemented in the **census**.

composing 構成する

　　Who are the Hispanics in America? They are generally
Spanish-speaking people from Latin America and their
10　descendants in America. They **refer to** ethnicity not race. Many
Hispanics identify themselves as Whites. The Hispanic
population **increase** is especially remarkable in the
southwestern **states** such as California, Texas, Arizona,
Nevada, and New Mexico. In Los Angeles, California in 2020,
15　47% of its population was Hispanics, 29% Whites, 12% Asians and
8% African American. Half a century ago, they were 17%, 61%,
3.6%, and 18% respectively. The same holds true in Houston,
Texas and Phoenix, Arizona. In these states, Whites are no
longer the simple majority in many schools and **workplaces**.
20　Spanish store signs in Hispanic communities are not rare in
these states as well as in Little Havana in Miami, Florida.

implemented
使用した
census 国勢調査

refer to ～
～のことを言う

increase 増加

states 州

workplaces 職場

　　The political world well reflects the rise in the Hispanic
population. In 2007, there were 29 Hispanic politicians in **the
U.S. Congress** composed of 535 in total. In 2022, it was 51. In
25　Nevada in February 2020, four Democratic **presidential
candidates** appealed their candidacies in Spanish. At the local
level, New Mexico has produced three Hispanic **governors**. In
2020, California had 40 Hispanic mayors and Texas 19. In
Texas, Beto O'Rourke, ex-Congressman, often **interacts** with
30　Hispanic voters in Spanish or uses Spanish on a website during
campaign events. A third of Texas residents speak Spanish. It is
essential for the politicians **ambitious** either in national or local
political spots to **heed** Hispanic voices and interests.

the U.S. Congress
アメリカ議会

**presidential
candidates**
大統領候補
governors 知事

interact 交流する

ambitious 望む
heed 注意する

　　Some project that the Hispanic population will continue to
35　**increase** both by immigration and by high birthrate and may
reach100 million in 2050! It may change the U.S. population

increase 増加する

makeup 構成

Ⅱ Listening Comprehension 42

Choose the correct answer about the passage.

1 A in the southwest

   B A third of them speak Spanish.

   C nineteen mayors in 2020

   D Beto O'Rourke is a politician in Texas.

2 A It was 47 percent.

   B fifty-one

   C forty

   D the same in Houston, Texas

3 A Little Havana is.

   B store signs written in Spanish

   C Yes, Miami is in the southwest of Florida.

   D school classes taught in Spanish

4 A It is a southwestern state.

   B There were 19 Hispanic mayors in 2020.

   C They had three Hispanic governors so far.

   D Many Hispanics live there.

Additional Listening Practice ⑭

Listen to two short conversations and choose the best answers for the questions.

1 A It is Monday.   B It closes at nine.

   C It is Saturday.   D Today is a weekday.

2 A She visited Sydney.   B for three weeks

   C Australia   D Yes, her second visit to Australia.

Ⅲ Writing ⑭ 否定

Exercise 1 ［　　］内の語（句）を並べ替え日本文にあう英文を書きなさい。
（注：句読点等は要適宜対応）

1 教室には居残りの生徒はほとんどいなかった。

[were, the classroom, left, students, there, in, few]

_____

2 我々には何故彼がめったに外出しないのかほとんど理解できない。

[why, seldom, out, hardly, can, goes, we, understand, he]

_____

3 今年の冬はあまり雪が降っていない。[snow, this, have, winter, had, we, little]

_____

Exercise 2 次の各日本文にあう英文を**否定の表現**に注意して書いてみましょう。

1 君はロック音楽が嫌いだね。僕もロックは嫌いだ。

→ _____

2 僕の友達は誰も車を持っていない。実際のところ、我々の誰も運転免許証を持っていないのです。

→ _____

3 子供の頃はクリスマスがとても（僕たちが）待ちきれなかったのを覚えています。

→ _____

Ⅳ TOEIC® ⑭
Incomplete Sentence → Reading Section の文中下線に入る適語（句）を選ぶ問題に挑戦しよう！

A word or phrase is missing in each of the sentences below. Select the best answer to complete the sentence.

1 Be sure to return the book I lent to you the other day when you ____ it. It belongs to our university library.

　　A　will have read　　B　read　　C　have read　　D　will read

2 Just ____ me to call Mr. Smith before leaving for London.

　　A　remember　　B　remembering　　C　remind　　D　recalling

3 Granting that the location is great, the rent of the apartment still seems to be a ____ expensive for its size.

　　A　considerably　　B　considerate　　C　considerable　　D　considering

4 ____ average the store has about fifty customers on weekdays.

　　A　With　　B　By　　C　For　　D　On

5 Although we tried every means ____, we were unable to find a solution to the problem.

　　A　imaginary　　B　imaginative　　C　imaginable　　D　imagination

Ⅴ Dialog ⑭ 43

Fill in the blanks.
(CD を聴き空白部分を書き取り暗記しましょう。)

[A：Japanese　B：American]

A：＿＿＿＿＿＿ ＿＿＿＿＿ ＿＿＿＿＿ ＿＿＿＿＿ ＿＿＿＿＿
＿＿＿＿＿？

B：Sure. ＿＿＿＿＿ ＿＿＿＿＿ ＿＿＿＿＿.

A：What does FMI stand for?

B：It stands for "For more information."

A：＿＿＿＿＿ ＿＿＿＿＿?

B：It means "For more information."

A：＿＿＿＿＿ ＿＿＿＿＿. Thank you so much.

B：＿＿＿＿＿ ＿＿＿＿＿.

Promenade 14

アメリカにおけるヒスパニック系の存在は、随所に見られる。

・Sonia Sotomayor（1954 年生誕）
　　ヒスパニック系（プエルトリコ系）女性初の最高
　　裁判所判事（2009 年）。

・Ellen Ochoa（1958 年生誕）
　　1993 年ヒスパニック系女性初の宇宙飛行士。祖父はメキシコ移民。

・Marco Rubio（1971 年生誕）
　　フロリダ州選出の連邦議会上院議員。キューバ移民の両親を持つマイアミ
　　生まれ。共和党のホープ。

・芸能界（歌手）
　Ricky Martin（1971 年生誕）
　　ラテンの貴公子の異名で知られる歌手。

・Gloria Estefan（1957 年生誕）
　　フロリダ州マイアミを拠点にする歌姫。キューバ難民の娘。難民からアメ
　　リカン・ドリームを体現化。

・Jennifer Lopez（1969 年生誕）
　　歌手、タレント

・プロスポーツ界
　　プロ野球　大リーグ Major League Baseball にも中南米出身の選手が多く所
　　　　属している。

I Passage Review

以下の 1〜14 の各文の下線部分に入る語（句）を選びなさい。

1 The American national flag, the Star-Spangled Banner, has _____ stars on it.

    A fifty   B thirteen   C red, blue and white   D national anthem

2 Las Vegas is _____ Washington D.C.

    A two hours behind   B three hours behind

    C four hours ahead of   D one hour ahead of

3 Los Angeles grew after _____ was discovered in the late 19th century.

    A gold mine   B Mexico   C Disneyland   D oil

4 There was once _____ on Ellis Island.

    A a national park   B a hospital for refugees from abroad

    C a port for a ferry to the Statue of Liberty

    D an immigration processing center

5 Times Square in New York is _____.

    A located at the southern edge of Manhattan Island   B near Wall Street

    C famous for the ball drop on the New Year's day

    D near Ground Zero, New York

6 Harvard University is _____.

    A the oldest college in America

    B located along Broadway in New York City

    C near Silicon Valley

    D releasing the data of COVID-19

7 Harvard University was founded to bring up _____.

    A nurses   B doctors   C teachers   D ministers

8 Pro-Choice supporters are _____.

    A against abortion   B called justices

    C among many state politicians   D for abortion

9 The Pulitzer Prize winners are announced at _____ in May every year.

    A five categories   B Stanford University

    C Columbia University   D Carnegie Hall

10 Among the immigrants America accepted in the 20th century was _____.

    A   Albert Einstein   B   Joseph Pulitzer

    C   Shuji Nakamura   D   Fred T. Korematsu

11 Slavery of Afro-Americans in America ended _____.

    A   when America declared independence in 1776

    B   in the mid 19th century

    C   in the mid 20th century

    D   in the South first

12 The Academy Awards ceremony has been mostly held in _____.

    A   New York   B   Los Angeles

    C   New York and Los Angeles alternately   D   Las Vegas

13 The Hispanics are those _____ and their descendants living in America.

    A   from Spain   B   from Latin America

    C   from Canada   D   born in Mexico

14 The GPA _____.

    A   includes the score of TOEFL-iBT

    B   is a degree required to enter a Law School

    C   can be a factor in job placement

    D   a high school transcript

Ⅱ Additional Exercises 44

1   Listening Practice

Part 1   Choose the best response to the question or statement.

1 A

    B

    C

2 A

    B

    C

3 A

    B

    C

4 A

    B

    C

5 A

    B

    C

Part 2　Listen to two short conversations and choose the best answers for the questions.

1　A　She'll be dating a Japanese man and she's a little nervous now.

　　B　She will be talking about some manners in Japan.

　　C　She is going to be one of the judges for a speech contest.

　　D　She will attend a seminar to learn Japanese manners.

2　A　It is quite old.

　　B　It was set at 40 degrees.

　　C　It was broken.

　　D　Nothing was wrong with it.

Ⅲ　Writing　⑮　it の用法／前置詞

Exercise 1　[　　]内の語（句）を並べ替え日本文にあう英文を書きなさい。
（注：句読点等は要適宜対応）

1　ある老婆が公園のベンチに座っていた。

[an, the park, was, the bench, old lady, on, sitting, in]

_____

2　我々は正午まで2時間、トムを門の所で待った。

[at, noon, two, for, we, hours, Tom, for, the gate, waited, until]

_____

3　昨日は雨だったが今日は晴れている。

[today, it, rainy, is, but, was, it, fine, yesterday]

_____

4　ここからそのバス停までどれくらいの距離ですか。

[to, here, is, far, stop, how, bus, from, the, it]

_____

Exercise 2　次の各日本文にあう英文を **it** と**前置詞**に注意して書いてみましょう。

1　この部屋はとても暑いです。外は騒がしいけど窓を開けてもいいですか。

　→ _____

2　我々がその事故を見たのは本当です。でも、私は、それについて何も言わない
　方がいいと思う。

　→ _____

3　私にとってその仕事を一日で終わらすのは容易ではない。

　→ _____

Incomplete Sentence → Reading Section の文中下線に入る適語 (句) を選ぶ問題に挑戦しよう！

A word or phrase is missing in each of the sentences below. Select the best answer to complete the sentence.

1 Today we have an American girl as our guest ＿＿＿ is staying with us this year as an exchange student from our sister high school in Hawaii.

      A whom   B who   C one   D whose

2 Everybody ＿＿＿ that Bob is an honest boy, but I don't think so.

      A is said   B says   C say   D are saying

3 The new book's author is delighted to learn that his book is selling quite ＿＿＿.

      A well   B fine   C good   D nice

4 The poor boy who was hit by a speeding car last night has ＿＿＿ hope of survival.

      A few   B only   C little   D hardly

5 What a small world! You are the ＿＿＿ person I expected to see here.

      A last   B least   C improper   D unusual

6 His request was cordially ＿＿＿.

      A turned off   B turned down   C put off   D pulled down

7 The professor instructed his students to ＿＿＿ their reports by the end of the month.

      A hand in   B hand out   C drop out   D drop in

8 The U.S. government ＿＿＿ strong displeasure over the Japanese government decision to overhaul the treaty.

      A held   B impressed   C expressed   D exploited

9 We don't expect to solve all the issues but to ＿＿＿ progress in some of them.

      A get   B have   C take   D make

10 When a company wants to reduce the number of its workers, it ＿＿＿ some of them.

      A kicks   B fires   C leaves   D pushes

アメリカと日本の概史

アメリカ	日　本（世界他）
1492年　コロンブス　新大陸（アメリカ）発見	
欧州主要国のアメリカ大陸進出が本格化	1573年　室町幕府滅亡　安土桃山（戦国）時代へ 1582年　本能寺の変
1603年	徳川家康江戸に幕府を開く
1607年　イギリス、現アメリカ東部にヴァージニア植民地建設 （1730年代までに東部に合計で13の植民地を建設）	
1619年　ヴァージニア植民地—黒人奴隷制導入、代議制による統治開始	参勤交代制度（1635年〜）
メイフラワー号プリマスに到着（1620年）	井原西鶴、松尾芭蕉ら活躍（1680年代〜）
1760年代　13州植民地と本国イギリス軋轢深まる	
1776年　アメリカ13植民地イギリスより独立を宣言	
1787年　合衆国憲法起草　批准（1788年）	
初代大統領にジョージ・ワシントン就任（1789年）、首都ニューヨーク	本居宣長「古事記伝」著す（1798年）
1801年　首都をワシントンDCに遷都	
1803年　フランスより西部ルイジアナ領地購入—アメリカ領土約2倍になる	
1823年　モンロー宣言。19世紀前半、南部で黒人奴隷制度の拡張堅固化が進む	水野忠邦　天保の改革（1841年）
1849年　サンフランシスコ近郊で金鉱発見（1848年）ゴールドラッシュ	
1850年代　黒人奴隷制度, 経済政策等をめぐり南部と北部の地域間軋轢が深刻化	ペリーの黒船浦賀に来航（1853年）
1861年　リンカーン大統領に就任、南北戦争（〜1865年）	（1854年日米和親条約を締結し開国。鎖国の終焉）
1863年　リンカーン大統領黒人奴隷解放宣言に署名	
1868年	明治維新（大政奉還1867年。江戸は東京に改称）
1896年　連邦最高裁「分離すれども平等」判決（黒人への人種差別容認、加速）	大日本帝国憲法公布（1889年）　日清戦争（1894年）
1898年　米西戦争（キューバがスペインより独立）	
アメリカ、フィリピンを支配下に置きアジア進出の拠点とする	日英同盟（1902年）　日露戦争（1904年）
1912年	大正元年　第1次世界大戦開戦1914）
1919年　禁酒法制定（合衆国憲法修正第18条）	第1次世界大戦終結／国際連盟加盟
1920年　女性に参政権	関東大震災（1923年）　普通選挙（1925年）
1929年　株価大暴落、大恐慌に突入	昭和元年（1926年）
1933年　フランクリン・ルーズベルト大統領就任—ニューディール政策推進	5・15事件（1932年）、　国際連盟脱退（1934年）
1939年	第二次世界大戦始まる。

	アメリカ	日 本（世界他）
1942 年	西海岸居住の日系アメリカ人強制収容所へ	ハワイの真珠湾急襲（1941 年 12 月）日米開戦へ
1945 年	第二次世界大戦終結	広島と長崎に原爆投下。日本国憲法公布（1946 年）
1954 年	ブラウン連邦最高裁判決（主に黒人への人種隔離・差別は違憲） 黒人への人種差別撤廃への運動高まる（～1965 年。キング牧師ら）	サンフランシスコ講和条約締結（1951年）日本独立と主権を回復 日米安全保障条約締結（同上年）
1963 年	ケネディ大統領テキサス州ダラスで暗殺される	
1965 年	主に黒人のための公民権法が成立(1964-65 年)	
1960 年	ベトナム戦争泥沼化（～1970 年代初期）	
1968 年	黒人運動指導者キング牧師暗殺される	東京オリンピック（1964 年）
1975 年	ニクソン大統領辞任	日中平和友好条約締結（1972 年）（米中国交正常化）
1989 年	ベルリンの壁崩壊、冷戦崩壊	平成元年
1990 年	湾岸戦争―アメリカがイラクへ侵攻	バブル崩壊
2000 年	大統領選で共和党ジョージ・ブッシュ候補大接戦で民主党ゴア氏を破る	金融危機（1990 年代）。IT（情報技術）時代黎明（同）
2001 年	ニューヨーク他同時多発テロ（9 月 11日）	
2005 年	アメリカ軍イラク侵攻―フセイン政権崩壊	小泉政権下で郵政民営化問う総選挙（自民党大勝）
2009 年	バラク・オバマ、初の黒人大統領に就任（2010 年 1 月）	参議院選挙で民主党大勝、自民党大敗
2011 年		東日本大震災（3 月 11 日）
2016 年	オバマ大統領広島訪問	安倍首相ハワイの真珠湾訪問。（英国ＥＵ離脱決定）
2017 年	ドナルド・トランプ大統領に就任（1 月）	
2020 年	COVID-19 Pandemic	新型コロナ パンデミック
2021 年	連邦議会堂襲撃（1 月 6 日）／ジョウ・バイデン大統領に就任	東京オリンピック（コロナ禍で前年から延期）岸田政権誕生
2022 年	ロシア　ウクライナに軍事侵攻	G7 サミット　広島で開催（2023 年）

アメリカの歴代大統領

	氏　名	在　任　期　間	所　属　政　党
初代	ジョージ・ワシントン	1789〜1797	
2代	ジョン・アダムズ	1797〜1801	フェデラリスト
3代	トーマス・ジェファソン	1801〜1809	＊民主・共和党 今日の民主党や共和党とは違う。
4代	ジェームズ・マディソン	1809〜1817	民主・共和党
5代	ジェームズ・モンロー	1817〜1825	民主・共和党
6代	ジョン・クィンシー・アダムズ	1825〜1829	民主・共和党
7代	アンドルー・ジャクソン	1829〜1837	民　主　党
8代	マーチン・バン・ビューレン	1837〜1841	民　主　党
9代	ウィリアム・ヘンリー・ハリソン	1841(就任1ヶ月後死去)	ウィッグ党
10代	ジョン・タイラー	1841〜1845	ウィッグ党・民主党
11代	ジェームズ・ポーク	1845〜1849	民　主　党
12代	ザガリー・テイラー	1849〜1850	ウィッグ党
13代	ミラード・フィルモア	1850〜1853	ウィッグ党
14代	フランクリン・ピアース	1853〜1857	民　主　党
15代	ジェームズ・ブキャナン	1857〜1861	民　主　党
16代	エイブラハム・リンカーン	1861〜1865(在任中暗殺される)	共　和　党
17代	アンドルー・ジョンソン	1865〜1869	共　和　党
18代	ユリアス・グラント	1869〜1877	共　和　党
19代	ラザフォード・ヘイズ	1877〜1881	共　和　党
20代	ジェームズ・ガーフィールズ	1881(在任中暗殺される)	共　和　党
21代	チェスター・アーサー	1881〜1885	共　和　党
22代/24代	グローバー・クリーブランド (連続ではない形で2期大統領を務めた)	1885〜1889/1893〜1897	民　主　党
23代	ベンジャミン・ハリソン	1889〜1893	共　和　党
24代	グローバー・クリーブランド (上記参照)	1893〜1897	民　主　党
25代	ウィリアム・マッキンリー	1897〜1901(在任中暗殺される)	共　和　党
26代	セオドア・ルーズベルト	1901〜1909	共　和　党
27代	ウィリアム・タフト	1909〜1913	共　和　党
28代	ウッドロー・ウィルソン	1913〜1921	民　主　党
29代	ウォレン・ハーディング	1921〜1923(任期途中死去)	共　和　党
30代	カルビン・クーリッジ	1923〜1929	共　和　党
31代	ハーバート・フーバー	1929〜1933	共　和　党
32代	フランクリン・ルーズベルト	1933〜1945(任期途中死去)	民　主　党
33代	ハリー・トルーマン	1945〜1953	民　主　党
34代	ドワイト・アイゼンハワー	1953〜1961	共　和　党
35代	ジョン・ケネディ	1961〜1963(在任中暗殺される)	民　主　党
36代	リンドン・ジョンソン	1963〜1969	民　主　党
37代	リチャード・ニクソン	1969〜1974(任期途中辞任)	共　和　党
38代	ジェラルド・フォード	1974〜1977	共　和　党
39代	ジミー・カーター	1977〜1981	民　主　党
40代	ロナルド・レーガン	1981〜1989	共　和　党
41代	ジョージ・ブッシュ	1989〜1993	共　和　党
42代	ビル・クリントン	1993〜2001	民　主　党
43代	ジョージ・ブッシュ (41代大統領と同名の息子)	2001〜2009	共　和　党
44代	バラク・オバマ	2009〜2017	民　主　党
45代	ドナルド・トランプ	2017〜2021	共　和　党
46代	ジョウ・バイデン	2021〜	民　主　党

テキストの音声は、弊社 HP　https://www.eihosha.co.jp/
の「テキスト音声ダウンロード」のバナーからダウンロードできます。
また、下記 QR コードを読み込み、音声ファイルをダウンロードするか、
ストリーミングページにジャンプして音声を聴くことができます。

A Glance at America
ちょっと見のアメリカ

2023 年 1 月 20 日　初　版

著　　者 ©　Jack　Brajcich
　　　　　谷　岡　敏　博

発　行　者　佐　々　木　元

発　行　所　株式会社　英　宝　社

〒 101-0032 東京都千代田区岩本町 2-7-7
電話 03-5833-5870　FAX03-5833-5872
https://www.eihosha.co.jp/

ISBN 978-4-269-42065-6 C1082
組版・印刷・製本／日本ハイコム株式会社